BEI

Nihil Obstat: Right Reverend Archimandrite Francis Vivona,
                S.T.M., J.C.L.

Imprimatur: Most Reverend Joseph A. Pepe, D.D., J.C.D.

Date: December 8, 2016
               The Immaculate Conception of the Blessed Virgin Mary

Excerpts from the New American Bible, revised edition Copyright © 2010, 1991, 1986, 1970 by the Confraternity of Christian Doctrine, Washington, D.C. Used with permission. All Rights Reserved. No part of the New American Bible may be reproduced in any form without permission in writing from the copyright owner.

Excerpts from Vatican Council II: The Conciliar and Post Conciliar Documents, New Revised Edition, edited by Austin Flannery, O.P., © 1996, Costello Publishing Co., Inc., Northport, NY are used by permission of the publisher, all rights reserved. No part of these excerpts may be reproduced, stored in a retrieval system, or transmitted in any form or by any means-electronic, mechanical, photocopying, recording or otherwise, without express permission of Costello Publishing Co.

ISBN 978-1-61796-221-9
Library of the Congress Control Number 2016956125
Artwork © 2017 Michael Adams, Licensee Aquinas Press
Text © 2017 Aquinas Press, Phoenix, Arizona
Printed in China

Table of Contents

Introduction 5
Mary, Model of the Church.. 6
Scriptures on Mary: The Old Testament....................... 8
Scriptures on Mary: The New Testament.................... 11
The Early Church, the Fathers, and Mary 21
The Doctors of the Church and Mary 23
St. Alphonsus Liguori and The Glories of Mary......... 24
Marian Feasts 27
Marian Prayers 28
Marian Devotions 30
May Devotions 31
The Brown Scapular 32
The Green Scapular 34
Devotion of the Three Hail Marys............................... 35
The Chaplet of the Ten Virtues 36
The Story of the Rosary 38
How to Pray the Rosary 40
Saint Louis de Montfort's Offering of the Rosary 41
The Prayers of the Rosary 42
The Mysteries of the Rosary 46
The Joyful Mysteries.. 49
The Luminous Mysteries 55
The Sorrowful Mysteries 61
The Glorious Mysteries.. 67
Our Lady of the Rosary 72
The Rosary Novena.. 73

The Apparitions of Mary	74
Our Lady of Guadalupe	77
Our Lady of the Miraculous Medal	85
Our Lady of Lourdes	91
Our Lady of Knock	95
Our Lady of Fatima	99
The Fatima Message and the First Saturday Devotion	105
Our Lady of Medjugorje	107
Our Lady of Kibeho	111
The Sorrows of Mary	117
The Promises of the Seven Sorrows	119
Meditations on the Seven Sorrows	121
Act of Consecration to Our Sorrowful Mother	135
Novena in Honor of Our Lady of Sorrows	136
Litany of Our Lady of Sorrows	140
The Angelus and Regina Coeli	144
Novenas	146
Novena to Our Lady of the Miraculous Medal	147
Novena to Our Lady of Mt. Carmel	153
Saint Louis de Montfort and the Consecration to Mary	158
The Saints and Mary	160
The Popes and the Rosary	164
St. John Paul II and Our Lady	167
Litany of the Blessed Virgin Mary	169
Our Lady of Perpetual Help	173
Novena to Our Lady of Perpetual Help	179
Padre Pio's Meditation Prayer on Mary Immaculate	185
A Final Word	191

Introduction

What is your greatest need right now? I would answer, "Hope." Hope that God will in fact work everything out for the good for those who love Him, as He has promised. Hope that we, His people, can continue to give His mercy to the world in our thoughts, words, and deeds. Hope that we can glorify Him as His Body, and live a life pleasing to Him, through Jesus Christ our Lord.

Of course, your answer may differ than mine. But one thing is certain: We all need God. And something else is certain: God has given us His Mother to help us come to Him.

It was when He was lifted high on the cross that Jesus said to Mary, "Woman, behold your son." And then to John, His beloved apostle, Jesus said, "Behold your mother." Jesus gave Mary the task of maternally forming every person ever created into His image, by the power of the Holy Spirit.

So, what is our greatest need? Perhaps it is to simply reach out to our Mother, to consecrate and entrust ourselves to her, so that she might bring us even closer to her Son, and help us to bring His presence, His love, His salvation, and His Divine Mercy, to every person for whom He died—and rose again.

Mary, Model of the Church

For God so loved the world that he gave his only Son, so that everyone who believes in him might not perish but might have eternal life.
-John 3:16

"'God sent forth his Son', but to prepare a body for him, he wanted the free co-operation of a creature. For this, from all eternity God chose for the mother of his Son a daughter of Israel, a young Jewish woman of Nazareth in Galilee, 'a virgin betrothed to a man whose name was Joseph, of the house of David; and the virgin's name was Mary'" (*Catechism of the Catholic Church*, [CCC] Par. 488).

In this seminal paragraph of the *Catechism of the Catholic Church*, the Church begins her presentation on the marvel of Mary, the Mother of God. Mary, a human being, nevertheless is intimately united to the Holy Trinity through God's absolutely gratuitous gift of grace to her and her own free and total cooperation with Him. More than any other created person, Mary believed in, hoped in, and loved God the Father, Son, and Holy Spirit. And the fantastic truth is, Mary is a prototype of the Church, of all believers, of all the children of God. What she is, we hope to be; where she has gone, we hope to follow.

But why is Mary so important for the world today? Mary's work did not finish with the birth, nor the death, nor the Resurrection, nor even with the Ascension of her Son into heaven. In fact, it was on the Cross that Jesus gave Mary her next great assignment. "When Jesus saw his mother and the disciple there whom he loved, he said to his mother, "Woman, behold, your son" (John 19:26).

Mary works for us through her "manifold intercession" in which she "continues to bring us the gifts of eternal salvation" (CCC par. 969). In other words, like any good mother, Mary is alert to see our needs and anxious to meet them, especially when they concern our salvation, the supernatural life of our souls. Mary wants to help restore this life for each one us, and to help it grow and prosper.

God wants to transform each of us into the image His Son. What an amazing desire of God! And He has willed that Mary help this happen through her Immaculate Heart, her suppliant heart that invokes God's power for His children, even when they are oblivious to their need for Him and His grace.

My children, for whom I am again in labor until Christ be formed in you!
-Galatians 4:19

Mary in the Old Testament

After the tragic disobedience of our first parents and their consequent fall from grace after the serpent's wily temptation in the Garden of Eden, the Lord God tells the serpent, "I will put enmity between you and the woman, and between your offspring and hers; He will strike at your head, while you strike at his heel" (Genesis 3:15).

The Church teaches that Mary "is already prophetically foreshadowed in the promise of victory over the serpent. ... Likewise she is the virgin who shall conceive and bear a son; whose name shall be called Emmanuel (see Isa 7:14; Mi 5:2-3; Mt 1:22-23)." (*Dogmatic Constitution of the Church*, [DCC] par. 55)

The enmity spoken of in the above Scripture is unending. Thus we need a permanent assistant in our fight to walk in the freedom of the Spirit that Jesus won for us. And that person is none other than our Lady, who has as one of her titles, "Our Lady of Perpetual Help." Likewise, if Eve, our first mother, had her part in our fall from grace, then Mary, the "new Eve" has her part in our new life in Christ.

But there's more. Besides the other Old Testament texts which refer and have been applied to Mary throughout the ages, there are also some outstanding

Old Testament women whose lives and stories prophetically foreshadow the Mother of God.

Sarah, the wife of Abraham, is a type of Mary, for she conceived Isaac, one of the Patriarchs of Israel, by a miracle of God's providence. "By faith he received power to generate, even though he was past the normal age—and Sarah herself was sterile—for he thought that the one who had made the promise was trustworthy" (Hebrews 11:11).

Miriam, Moses' sister, also foreshadows Mary in her action of preserving Moses from the death that Pharaoh tried to inflict on all Hebrew baby boys. Mary protected the infant Jesus and helped spirit Him away to Egypt, far from the clutches of the raging Herod. Miriam also sang a mighty song of praise and thanksgiving to God, as did Mary in her beautiful *Magnificat*.

Judith was a lovely and God-fearing widow in Israel. Yet God used her to defeat Holofernes, a Chaldean general who had laid siege to a city of Israel. The people praised Judith singing, "You are the glory of Jerusalem, the surpassing joy of Israel; You are the splendid boast of our people" (Judith 15:9). Likewise, Mary crushed the head of the evil one, and freed us from the dominion of sin.

Mary in the New Testament

The New Testament proclaims the good news of Jesus Christ. But it all starts with the Annunciation of the angel Gabriel to Mary that God has chosen her to be the mother of His Son. This unique moment is pregnant with expectation: Mary is a young Jewish virgin with a free will. She can either accept or decline God's astounding invitation. She says simply, "Behold, I am the handmaid of the Lord. May it be done to me according to your word" (Luke 1:38), and the Incarnation occurs.

Scarcely had the angel departed than Mary herself left "in haste" to visit her cousin, Elizabeth, whom God had miraculously allowed to become pregnant in her old age. When Elizabeth heard Mary's greeting, "the infant leaped in her womb, and Elizabeth, filled with the holy Spirit, cried out in a loud voice and said, "Most blessed are you among women, and blessed is the fruit of your womb. And how does this happen to me, that the mother of my Lord should come to me? For at the moment the sound of your greeting reached my ears, the infant in my womb leaped for joy. Blessed are you who believed that what was spoken to you by the Lord would be fulfilled" (Luke 1:41-45).

In Elizabeth's response, we see the Holy Spirit

prophetically signaling to us a key attribute of Mary: she is one who believes; hence, she is blessed, for the Lord will fulfill His word.

Mary is the Immaculate Conception. We know this by her own revelation at Lourdes, but also by the infallible teaching of the Church in declaring this dogma. Beginning from this sublime state of innocence, Mary continued to please the Father, ever obedient to Him. Thus, when He speaks, she listens with faith, fully confident that He will fulfill His word completely, regardless of circumstances to the contrary.

Mary responds to Elizabeth's greeting with her *Magnificat* (Luke 1:46-55), a beautiful hymn of praise and blessing to God. She remains with Elizabeth for three months, and then returns home. Joseph, Mary's fiancé, takes her into his home after being instructed by an angel in his dream. They journey six months later to Bethlehem for the census, and there Mary "gave birth to her firstborn son. She wrapped him in swaddling clothes and laid him in a manger, because there was no room for them in the inn" (Luke 2:7).

That very night an angel appeared to shepherds keeping watch over their flocks in nearby fields, announcing,

"'Do not be afraid; for behold, I proclaim to you

good news of great joy that will be for all the people. For today in the city of David a savior has been born for you who is Messiah and Lord. And this will be a sign for you: you will find an infant wrapped in swaddling clothes and lying in a manger.' And suddenly there was a multitude of the heavenly host with the angel, praising God and saying: 'Glory to God in the highest and on earth peace to those on whom his favor rests'" (Luke 2:10-14).

After eight days, Mary and Joseph had the baby circumcised, and "he was named Jesus, the name given him by the angel before he was conceived in the womb" (Luke 2:21). Then, 40 days after the birth of Jesus, Mary and Joseph took Him to the Temple in Jerusalem, to present Him to the Lord, according to the prescription of the Law. There they met old Simeon. "This man was righteous and devout, awaiting the consolation of Israel, and the holy Spirit was upon him. It had been revealed to him by the holy Spirit that he should not see death before he had seen the Messiah of the Lord"
(Luke 2:25-26). Simeon took the child in his arms, and blessed God, saying,

"Now, Master, you may let your servant go in peace,

according to your word, for my eyes have seen your salvation, which you prepared in sight of all the peoples, a light for revelation to the Gentiles, and glory for your people Israel" (Luke 2:29-32).

Joseph and Mary were amazed at all this. Simeon blessed them and then said to Mary, "'Behold, this child is destined for the fall and rise of many in Israel, and to be a sign that will be contradicted (and you yourself a sword will pierce) so that the thoughts of many hearts may be revealed'" (Luke 2:34-35).

Simeon confirms the word of the angel and the glory of God's Messiah; however, he also reminds Mary and Joseph of the Suffering Servant prophecies of Isaiah (See Isaiah 52:13—53:12). Simeon then prophesies to Mary that she too will suffer a sword through her heart, in a sort of mystical union with her Son's destiny.

Did Mary fully understand all these events and the words spoken to her? Possibly not. But she did receive them all, "reflecting on them in her heart" (Luke 2:19). So we see that in addition to her faith, Mary had a sensitive and perceptive heart, a listening heart, a quiet and meditative heart. This is one amazing woman!

The New Testament goes on to document the arrival of the Magi, who found the child Jesus "with

Mary his mother" (Matthew 2:11), and worshipped Him. Then Herod tried to kill the infant King, but Joseph, warned in a dream, "rose and took the child and his mother by night and departed for Egypt" (Matthew 2:14). After the death of Herod, they returned home to Nazareth.

When Jesus was 12, the Holy Family journeyed to Jerusalem for the Passover, but Jesus stayed behind, only to be found after three days of anxious searching by Mary and Joseph. When Mary reproved Jesus, He replied somewhat cryptically, "Why were you looking for me? Did you not know that I must be in my Father's house?" (Luke 2:49). He then returned home with them, "and was obedient to them; and his mother kept all these things in her heart" (Luke 2:51).

We next hear of Mary at the Wedding Feast at Cana, as Jesus is beginning His public ministry. The hosts run out of wine, and Mary brings the need to Jesus. He responds, again rather enigmatically, "Woman, how does your concern affect me? My hour has not yet come" (John 2:4). Nonetheless, Mary directs the servants, "Do whatever he tells you" (John 2:5). They follow His instructions to fill 6 stone jars with water, and Jesus turns the water into enough wine for several weddings! We see the trust brimming in Mary's heart lead to a birth of faith in His followers, for upon seeing this, Jesus' disciples began to believe in Him.

As Jesus continued His ministry, Mary and some relatives went to see Him one day. When Jesus was told they were outside, He responded, "'Who are my mother and (my) brothers?' And looking around at those seated in the circle he said, 'Here are my mother and my brothers. (For) whoever does the will of God is my brother and sister and mother'" (Mark 3:33-35).

Another time, while Jesus was teaching, a woman in the crowd called out, "'Blessed is the womb that carried you and the breasts at which you nursed.' He replied, 'Rather, blessed are those who hear the word of God and observe it'" (Luke 11:27-28).

At first glance, it seems that Jesus spoke pretty directly to or about His Mother, and that He didn't mince words. But upon further reflection, it appears that He was perhaps allowing Mary to be a teaching instrument for our sakes. Jesus is teaching us that the Kingdom is not just an improved state of our natural life, but is instead a new life with new priorities, God being the first.

We next see Mary standing beneath the cross of Jesus, with the apostle John, Mary the wife of Clopas, and Mary Magdalene. When Jesus saw them there, He said to his mother, "Woman, behold, your son." He then said to John, "Behold, your mother." (John 19:26, 27). From that hour, the beloved disciple took Mary into his home.

The New Testament is silent about Mary after the crucifixion itself, though long-standing tradition, reflected in the Stations of the Cross and in the sense of the faithful, is that Mary held the body of her Son Jesus after He was taken down from the cross and that she helped lay Him to rest in the tomb.

Likewise, some of the early Church Fathers, such as Saint John Chrysostom and Saint Jerome, teach that Mary was indeed at the tomb and that Jesus appeared to her first after His Resurrection from the dead.

The final direct mention of Mary in the New Testament is in Acts 1:13-15, where the apostles, who are gathered in the upper room in Jerusalem, "devoted themselves with one accord to prayer, together with some women, and Mary the mother of Jesus, and his brothers" (Acts 1:14).

Out of this prayer, in the same room a few days later, is born the incredible Pentecost experience of the descent of the Holy Spirit on these first believers, and the birth of the Church.

While the Book of Acts records the final *physical* mention of Mary, Saint John the Apostle writes in the final book of Scripture: "A great sign appeared in the sky, a woman clothed with the sun, with the moon under her feet, and on her head a crown of twelve stars. She was with child and wailed aloud in pain as she labored to give birth" (Revelation 12:1-2). A fearful dragon—Satan—stands before the woman as she is about to deliver her child, that he might devour it. The woman gives birth to a son, one destined to rule all the nations, who is caught up to heaven while the woman herself flees to a place prepared for her by God.

The remainder of this chapter from the Book of Revelation is taken up with an awesome description of the dragon—Satan—as he seeks to destroy the woman's child, and, failing that, moves on to war against the woman and her offspring.

What does all this mean? Church teaching is silent here except that many do see in this woman an image of Mary and of the Church, laboring to give birth to the Body of Christ, which is destined, as Saint John the Evangelist asserts and Saint Paul affirms, to judge and rule all nations.

The Early Church, the Fathers, and Mary

First and foremost, as is right and just, the members of the Early Church focused on Jesus Christ their Lord and Savior. They worshipped and grew in their adoration of Him as the Son of the Living God.

Even so, history records a veneration for Mary that budded forth from the evident seeds of love for her from the beginning of the Christian Faith. Late first-century frescoes in the Roman catacombs depict Mary, with and without her Son. One of them, in the catacombs of Saint Agnes, shows a woman whose arms are raised in prayer with a child sitting in front of her, with both mother and child gazing out at the viewer. This painting is regarded by many as an early Madonna and Child.

Meanwhile, in the East, churches dedicated to Mary thrived, such as Our Lady of Tortosa—the first church built by Saint Peter the Apostle in Mary's honor in the city of Tartus, Syria. In 130 AD, the early Church Father Irenaeus wrote of Mary as the "Second Eve," who through her obedience, helped to save a world that had been lost through the first Eve's disobedience.

The oldest prayer to Mary, *Sub Tuum Praesidium* (250 A.D.), was prayed by the faithful seeking Mary's intercession for protection and deliverance. (See page 29.) Less than 200 years later, at the Council of Ephesus, the Church formally declared Mary to be the *Theotokos*—God-bearer—or "Mother of God." This led to an extraordinary flourishing of devotion and love for the Blessed Virgin Mary throughout all of Christendom. *Lumen Gentium*, the Vatican II document on the Church, states:

> Accordingly, following the Council of Ephesus, there was a remarkable growth in the cult of the People of God towards Mary, in veneration and love, in invocation and imitation, according to her own prophetic words: "all generations shall call me blessed, because he that is mighty hath done great things to me" (Lk 1:48) (*Lumen Gentium*, No. 66).

The early Church Fathers give us a good number of affirmations for Mary, including this from Saint Gregory Thaumaturgus: "You are the vessel and tabernacle containing all mysteries. You know what the Patriarchs never knew; you have experienced what was never revealed to the Angels; you have heard what the Prophets never heard. In a word, all that was hidden from preceding generations was made known to you; even more, most of these wonders depended on you."

The Doctors of the Church and Mary

Over the years, the Church continued to grow in its understanding and experience of Mary as the Mother of Jesus and our Mother as well. As with her Son, there are many dimensions of Mary, not the least of which is her two roles: first of all as Mother of Jesus but then, as Mother of His Church, a role Jesus gave her from the cross when He said, "Woman, behold your son."

The Church gives the title of "Doctor" to a very select group of saints, whose writings and teachings have proven to be useful to believers "in any age of the Church." These Doctors, three of whom are women, are particularly renowned for their deep understanding and orthodox teaching of the Faith.

O sinner, be not discouraged, but have recourse to Mary in all your necessities. Call her to your assistance, for such is the divine Will that she should help in every kind of necessity.
– Saint Basil the Great

It is impossible to save one's soul without devotion to Mary and without her protection.
– Saint Anselm

In trial or difficulty I have recourse to Mother Mary, whose glance alone is enough to dissipate every fear.
– Saint Therese of Lisieux

The Glories of Mary
-Saint Alphonsus Liguori

Saint Alphonsus Liguori (1696-1787) was a remarkable man—a gifted lawyer, priest, servant of the poor, founder of the Redemptorist Order, artist, composer, writer, preacher, moral theologian, and Bishop. He preached the love of God, the love that redeems us, heals us, and makes us new. In God, Saint Alphonsus asserted, love and freedom come together. Like the Prodigal Son, our response to God ought to be one, not of fear, but of gratitude and surprise at a Father who always welcomes us back and clothes us with His rich robes of mercy.

Saint Alphonsus had a deep and devoted love for Mary, who was a fountain of spiritual life and consolation for him. In all his many challenges, he found in her a loving Mother, helper, and guide. During his lifetime, certain writers ridiculed devotion to Mary, and Saint Alphonsus responded with a magnificent work, *The Glories of Mary*.

His original book is in two parts. In the first part, Alphonsus presents a striking commentary on the prayer of the *Hail Holy Queen*. In the second, he discusses the principal feasts of Our Lady, her Seven Sorrows, and her ten great virtues. Saint Alphonsus closes the book with a grand and comprehensive collection of Marian prayers, meditations, and devotions. He gives numerous citations on devotion to Mary from Holy Scriptures, the Liturgy, Church Fathers, Doctors of the Church, Saints, and Popes, along with his own views on veneration to this handmaid of the Lord.

According to Redemptorist Father Sabatino Majorano, professor at Rome's Alphonsianum Institute, *The Glories of Mary* is "written with the heart more than the head, though it is intelligent." Father Majorano also stresses that the two focal points of Saint Alphonsus were "the crucifix as an expression of God's love—not His justice—and Mary." He noted that Saint Alphonsus focused on the role of Mary as "Queen of Mercy." She is "God's welcomer .... So, her mercy is acceptance and her mercy is her ability to intercede for us and her mercy is to always anticipate our needs, like she did at the wedding at Cana."

The spear which opened his side passed through the soul of the Virgin, which could not be torn from the heart of Jesus.
– Saint Bernard, as quoted in *The Glories of Mary*

Marian Feasts
Major Feasts of Our Lady

January 1: Mary, Mother of God
February 2: The Presentation of the Lord
February 11: Our Lady of Lourdes
March 25: The Annunciation
May: The Month of Mary
May 13: Our Lady of Fatima
Saturday following the feast of Corpus Christi: The Immaculate Heart of Mary
May 31: The Visitation of Mary
July 16: Our Lady of Mount Carmel
August 5: Dedication of the Basilica of St. Mary Major
August 15: The Assumption of the Blessed Virgin Mary
August 22: The Queenship of Mary
September 8: The Nativity of Mary
September 12: The Holy Name of Mary
September 15: Our Lady of Sorrows
October: The Month of the Rosary
October 7: Our Lady of the Rosary
November 21: The Presentation of Mary
December 8: The Immaculate Conception
December 12: Our Lady of Guadalupe
December 25: The Nativity of the Lord
First Sunday after Christmas: The Holy Family

Marian Prayers

The Magnificat

"My soul proclaims the greatness of the Lord;
my spirit rejoices in God my savior.
For he has looked upon his handmaid's lowliness;
behold, from now on will all ages call me blessed.
The Mighty One has done great things for me,
and holy is his name.
His mercy is from age to age
to those who fear him.
He has shown might with his arm,
dispersed the arrogant of mind and heart.
He has thrown down the rulers from their thrones
but lifted up the lowly.
The hungry he has filled with good things;
the rich he has sent away empty.
He has helped Israel his servant,
remembering his mercy,
according to his promise to our fathers,
to Abraham and to his descendants forever."
– Luke 1:45-55

Sub Tuum Praesidium

The oldest Marian prayer in the Church is known as the *Sub Tuum*, from the first two words of the prayer in Latin.

> We fly to your patronage,
> O holy Mother of God;
> despise not our prayers in our necessities,
> but deliver us always from all dangers,
> O glorious and blessed Virgin.

This prayer dates back to third century Egypt, when Christians were suffering under intense Roman persecution. Interestingly, the Coptic Christians of Egypt began calling Mary "Mother of God" long before the Council of Ephesus officially endorsed this title for Mary in 431.

Alma Redemptoris

Loving Mother of the Redeemer, gate of heaven, star of the sea, assist your people who have fallen yet strive to rise again. To the wonderment of nature you bore your Creator, yet remained a virgin after as before. You who received Gabriel's joyful greeting, have pity on us poor sinners. Amen.

Marian Devotions

History reveals the early and amazing growth of Marian devotion in all parts of the Church, as in every age believers have turned to Our Lady for protection, provision, hope, and help. They are triumphant witnesses that Our Lady has never left unaided anyone who has fled to her protection, implored her help, or sought her intercession.

Like her Son Jesus, Mary will never forsake us. Small wonder, then, that the saints all agree that devotion to Mary is a great sign of God's providence. The popes, the shepherds of our Church, have consistently held up our Blessed Mother as the first among the disciples and Mother of the Church. Marian Devotions to the Virgin Mary have always helped believers to grow closer to Mary and her Son, our Savior Jesus Christ. *The Dogmatic Constitution on the Church* proclaims:

> The various forms of piety toward the Mother of God, which the Church ... has approved, bring it about that while the Mother is honored, the Son, through whom all things have their being (cf. Col. 1:15-16) and in whom it has pleased the Father that all fullness should dwell, (cf. Col. 1:19) is rightly known, loved and glorified and that all His commands are observed (par. 66).

May Devotions to Mary

In the late 1700's, a Roman Jesuit began the practice of dedicating the month of May to Our Lady. This devotion spread to the entire Church, and has become a regular part of Catholic life.

In May, many churches pray the Rosary daily. Some crown Our Lady's statue with a wreath of blossoms to indicate Mary's virtues. In some parishes or neighborhoods, the faithful carry Our Lady's statue in a May procession while singing Marian hymns.

A great way to honor Mary as a family is to set up a May altar at home. Place a statue of Our Lady in your living room and make a little shrine decorated with flowers. Then gather nightly to pray all or part of the Family Rosary.

Another distinctive way to honor Our Lady is to build an outdoor Marian shrine. Obtain a concrete or fiberglass statue, and place it on a large rock or in a grotto. If you wish you may plant a Mary Garden around the shrine. Be sure to include roses in honor of the Mystical Rose! During May, try to grow in your love for Mary. Let her be your Mother. Talk to her. Consecrate your heart to her Immaculate and Motherly Heart. Let Mary lead you to her Son, Jesus, which she loves to do!

The Brown Scapular

According to tradition, over 700 years ago Our Blessed Mother appeared to Saint Simon Stock, holding out to him a brown woolen scapular. "Receive, my beloved son, the Scapular of thy Order, as a distinctive sign of my Confraternity. Whoever dies invested with this Scapular shall be preserved from the eternal flames. It is a sign of salvation, a sure safeguard in danger, a pledge of peace and of my special protection until the end of the ages."

The Brown Scapular, then, is a special garment worn as a sign of love and devotion to Mary our

Mother and Queen. It consists of two small pieces of cloth, typically wool, connected by two long cords worn over the head and resting on the shoulders. We are called to wear the scapular continuously, to observe chastity according to our state in life (married/single), and to pray daily the *Little Office of the Blessed Virgin Mary* or do any of the following:

- Observe the fasts of the Church.
- Pray five decades of the Holy Rosary.
- Do a good work with the permission of a priest.

A priest typically enrolls members into the Scapular Confraternity. Saint John Paul II wrote: "The most genuine form of devotion to the Blessed Virgin, expressed by the humble sign of the Scapular, is consecration to her Immaculate Heart."

To wear the brown scapular is to trust in Our Lady, who has great power of intercession before her Son, and to receive her continuous protection.

The Green Scapular

In 1840, ten years after Our Lady gave to Saint Catherine Labouré the Miraculous Medal, she began appearing to a young nun of the same convent, Sister Justine Bisqueyburu. Our Lady held in her right hand her heart, surrounded by fire, and emanating brilliant rays. In her left hand she held a scapular consisting of a single piece of green cloth on a green cord.

On one side of the scapular was a picture of Mary as she had appeared to Sister Justine; on the other was a heart inflamed with rays more brilliant than the sun and clearer than crystal. This heart was surrounded by the words: Immaculate Heart of Mary, pray for us now and at the hour of our death. Sister Justine understood that this new scapular would contribute to the conversion of sinners, helping them receive the grace of a happy death, and that the faithful were to distribute it with confidence.

Practices:
- Have a priest bless the scapular, and wear or carry it.
- Put it in someone's room to help them.
- Pray daily: "Immaculate Heart of Mary, pray for us now and at the hour of our death."

Devotion of the Three Hail Marys for a Happy Death

One of the surest marks of God's favor and a most powerful means of salvation is devotion to Our Blessed Mother Mary. All the Doctors of the Church unanimously proclaim this, as does Saint Alphonsus Liguori: "The devoted servant of Mary will never perish."

Centuries ago, Our Lady appeared to Saint Matilde of Germany, saying to her, "I have a little key that will open the door of heaven for you when you die. All you have to do is to say, in my honor, three Hail Marys, every day."

Saint Anthony of Padua was the first to practice and preach this, honoring Mary for her virginity and keeping a clean mind, heart, and body. Through his example he invited many others to live virtuously. Other saints affirm this devotion, which brings many graces during life and at the hour of death.

This devotion carries a partial indulgence for all those who pray the three Hail Marys morning and evening, adding Saint Alphonsus' plea: "O Mary, Mother of mine, protect me from mortal sin through this day (night)."

The Chaplet of the Ten Virtues

Early in the 16th century, Saint Joanne de Valois and Blessed Gilbert OFM, founded the Sisters of the Annunciation of the Blessed Virgin Mary. Blessed Gilbert composed a rule based on the ten Evangelical virtues of Mary, and Saint Joanne composed a chaplet based on the rule.

The chaplet is comprised of ten beads—typically black—with a crucifix on one end and a medal with an image of Mary Immaculate on the other. It has been passed on by tradition in the Marian Order and is approved by the Church.

Begin with the Sign of the Cross, then pray five decades of one *Our Father* each followed by ten *Hail Mary's*. After praying the words "Holy Mary, Mother of God" mention one virtue, in the following order:

1. Most pure,
2. Most prudent,
3. Most humble,
4. Most faithful,
5. Most devout,
6. Most obedient,
7. Most poor,
8. Most patient,
9. Most merciful,
10. Most sorrowful,

. . . pray for us sinners now and at the hour of our death."

V. Glory to the Father and to the Son and to the Holy Spirit.
R. As it was in the beginning, is now and will be forever. Amen.
V. In Your Conception, O Virgin Mary, You were Immaculate.
R. Pray for us to the Father whose son, Jesus, you brought forth into the world.

Let us pray:
Father, you prepared the Virgin Mary to be the worthy mother of your Son. You let her share beforehand in the salvation Christ would bring by His death, and kept her sinless from the first moment of her conception. Help us by her prayers to live in Your presence without sin. We ask this in the name of Jesus the Lord. Amen.

V. The Virgin Mary's Immaculate Conception
R. Be our Health and our Protection. Amen.

The Story of the Rosary

The word *Rosary–rosarium–*means *of roses*. A Rosary, then, is a *crown of roses*, with each prayer being a single rose that we give to Mary. Early Christian hermits daily prayed the 150 Psalms, keeping count with rocks or beads. Irish monks later divided the psalms into three groups of 50 and printed them as *The Psalter*, which enabled them to pray the Psalms communally.

The *Glory Be* was always prayed with the Psalms. In time, the monks substituted the *Our Father* for each Psalm. By 1000 AD, *The Little Psalter*, a book of 150 *Our Fathers* with meditations, began to circulate. Gradually, the Our Fathers were replaced with *Aves*— the angelic salutation to Mary and the greeting of Elizabeth.

According to tradition, Our Lady appeared to Saint Dominic in 1208 and told him to "preach my Psalter composed of 150 *Aves* and 15 *Our Fathers*." By the 16th century, people were meditating on the mysteries of Jesus, while praying their *Aves*.

In 1563, the Council of Trent handed down the second half of the *Hail Mary*. *The Salve Regina*, affirming Mary's role as Queen of Heaven and Earth, came next, followed by the *Apostles' Creed*. On October 7, 1573, after a miraculous naval victory at the Battle of Lepanto credited to the power of the Rosary, Pope Gregory XIII established the Feast of the Holy Rosary.

Pope Leo XIII, who shepherded the Church from 1878-1903, wrote twelve encyclicals and numerous letters on the Rosary, touching upon all its aspects and leading to a resurgence of its devotion. Through the Rosary, the pope attested, we can most quickly and easily reach Mary, and through her, Jesus.

In 1917, Mary appeared to three young children at Fatima. Referring to herself as the Lady of the Rosary, she begged all Christians to pray the Rosary daily as a powerful weapon for world peace. Mary taught the children the *Fatima Prayer*, to be prayed after the *Glory Be*.

With the heartfelt cry, **"The family that prays together stays together!"** Father Patrick Peyton founded the Family Rosary Crusade in 1942. Father Peyton believed that world peace flowed from peace in each heart and family—and the key was family prayer, especially the Rosary.

Pope Pius XII encouraged the Family Rosary, as did his successors, most notably Saint John Paul II, who wrote his apostolic letter, *The Rosary of the Virgin Mary*, in October, 2002. In his letter the Pope added five new mysteries of Light—the Luminous Mysteries—to the Rosary, and initiated a Year of the Rosary.

Meditation on the 20 Mysteries, or scenes, from the life of Jesus and Mary remains at the heart of this time-honored and much beloved prayer to Our Lady.

How to Pray the Rosary

- Make the *Sign of the Cross* and pray the *Apostles' Creed*, while holding the crucifix.
- Pray one *Our Father* on the first bead, three *Hail Marys* on the next three beads for the virtues of Faith, Hope, and Charity, and finish with a *Glory Be*.
- Announce the first Mystery. Pause for a moment to reflect on it. Then pray an *Our Father* on the large bead, ten *Hail Marys* on the smaller beads, and finish with a *Glory Be*. This is one decade.
- If you wish, you may pray the *Fatima Prayer*, found on page 43.
- Continue in this way until you have prayed all five decades. To finish, pray the *Hail Holy Queen*.
- You may wish to pray the *Prayers after the Rosary*, found on page 44.

Saint Louis de Montfort's Offering of the Rosary

I unite with all the saints in Heaven, with all the just on earth and with all the faithful here present. I unite with Thee, O my Jesus, in order to praise worthily Thy holy Mother and to praise Thee in her and through her. I renounce all the distractions I may have during this Rosary, which I wish to say with modesty, attention, and devotion, just as if it were to be the last of my life.

We offer Thee, O Most Holy Trinity, this Creed in honor of all the mysteries of our Faith; this Our Father and these three Hail Marys in honor of the unity of Thy Essence and the Trinity of Thy Persons. We ask of Thee a lively faith, a firm hope and an ardent charity. Amen.

The Prayers of the Rosary

The Apostles' Creed

I believe in God, the Father Almighty, Creator of heaven and earth; and in Jesus Christ, His only Son, our Lord, Who was conceived by the Holy Spirit, born of the Virgin Mary, suffered under Pontius Pilate, was crucified, died, and was buried.

He descended into hell; the third day He rose from the dead. He ascended into heaven, and is seated at the right hand of God, the Father Almighty; from thence He shall come to judge the living and the dead.

I believe in the Holy Spirit, the Holy Catholic Church, the communion of saints, the forgiveness of sins, the resurrection of the body, and life everlasting. Amen.

Our Father

Our Father, Who art in heaven, hallowed be Thy Name; Thy Kingdom come; Thy Will be done on earth as it is in heaven. Give us this day our daily bread; and forgive us our trespasses, as we forgive those who trespass against us; and lead us not into temptation, but deliver us from evil. Amen.

Hail Mary

Hail Mary, full of grace, the Lord is with thee; blessed art thou among women, and blessed is the fruit of thy womb, Jesus.

Holy Mary, Mother of God, pray for us sinners, now and at the hour of our death. Amen.

Glory Be

Glory be to the Father, and to the Son, and to the Holy Spirit; as it was in the beginning, is now, and ever shall be, world without end. Amen.

Fatima Prayer

O my Jesus, forgive us our sins; save us from the fires of hell. Lead all souls to Heaven, especially those most in need of Your mercy.

Hail, Holy Queen

Hail, Holy Queen, Mother of Mercy, Our life, our sweetness, and our hope! To thee do we cry, poor banished children of Eve; to thee do we send up our sighs, mourning and weeping in this valley of tears. Turn then, most gracious advocate, thine eyes of mercy toward us; and after this our exile show unto us the blessed fruit of thy womb, Jesus; O clement, O loving, O sweet Virgin Mary.

V. Pray for us, O holy Mother of God,
R. That we may be made worthy of the promises of Christ.

Prayer After the Rosary

O God, whose only-begotten Son, by His life, death and resurrection, has purchased for us the rewards of eternal life; grant, we beseech Thee, that, meditating upon these mysteries of the Most Holy Rosary of the Blessed Virgin Mary, we may imitate what they contain and obtain what they promise, through the same Christ our Lord. Amen.

Memorare

Remember, O most gracious Virgin Mary, that never was it known, that anyone who fled to thy protection, implored thy help or sought thy intercession, was left unaided. Inspired by this confidence, I fly unto thee, O Virgin of virgins my Mother; to thee do I come, before thee I stand, sinful and sorrowful. O Mother of the Word Incarnate, despise not my petitions, but in thy mercy hear and answer me. Amen.

Daily Consecration to Mary

O Mary, my Queen and my Mother, I give myself entirely to you. And as proof of my filial devotion, I consecrate to you this day my eyes, my ears, my mouth, my heart, my whole being without reserve. Therefore, good Mother, as I am your own, keep me and guard me as your property and possession. Amen.

Prayer for the Faithful Departed
May the Souls of the Faithful Departed, through the mercy of God, rest in peace. Amen.

The Mysteries of the Rosary

A mystery of faith is a supernatural truth which cannot be known except by God's revelation. As we pray the Rosary, a *compendium* of the Gospel, we contemplate the Christian mystery by meditating on twenty events, or mysteries, in the lives of Jesus and His Blessed Mother.

We pray the Joyful Mysteries on Mondays and Saturdays. With Mary we remember the wonderful event of the Incarnation and the joy radiating from it.

We pray the Luminous Mysteries, the Mysteries of Light, on Thursdays. With Mary we consider how Jesus, the Light of the world, proclaimed the Gospel of the Kingdom during His public ministry.

We pray the Sorrowful Mysteries on Tuesdays and Fridays. With Mary we contemplate the Passion and Death of Jesus—the fullness of the revelation of God's love.

We pray the Glorious Mysteries on Wednesdays and Sundays. With Mary we remember and reflect on the life of the Risen Christ, the gift of the Holy Spirit, and Mary's glory in heaven. In so doing, we rediscover the reasons for our own faith and relive the joy of Mary and the disciples.

Meditation and the Mysteries

It is best to pause a moment after announcing each Rosary mystery in order to reflect on it, apply it to ourselves, and formulate an intention for it. On the following pages you will find each mystery, followed by an intention, a scripture verse, a meditation, an application, and a prayer of intercession.

To meditate on the mysteries of the Rosary, reflect on each event as presented in the Scriptures. Place yourself in each scene; see what the characters see, hear what they hear, be as present as possible. In so doing allow the Holy Spirit to touch your heart.

Next, apply the mystery to your own life. How does this mystery affect me? What is the Lord asking me to do? With Jesus and Mary as my models, what lessons can I take for my day today? Ask God to forgive your failures and thank Him for His victories in you. Invite Him to transform you, through the intercession of your Mother, into the image of His Son.

Finally, as you pray each mystery, intercede for others. Stand in the gap and pray for those in the Body of Christ and in our world today who are most in need of God's mercy, grace, and peace.

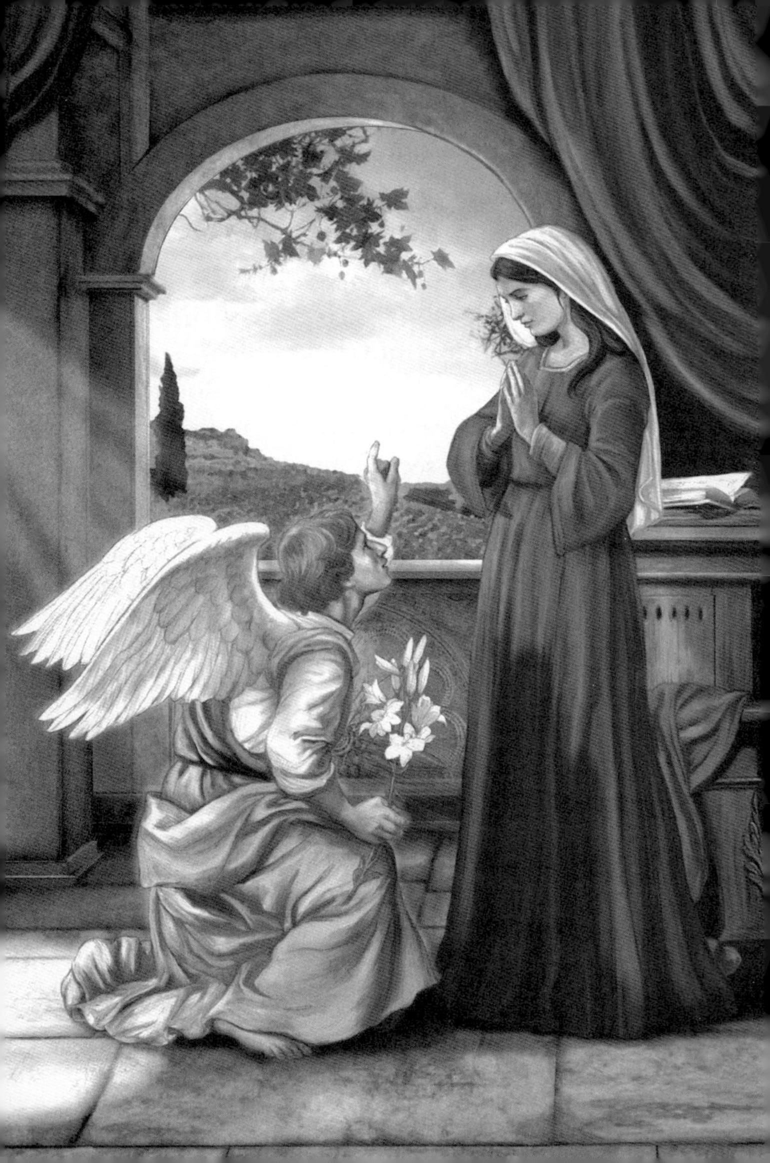

The Joyful Mysteries
The Annunciation
Humility

"Do not be afraid, Mary, for you have found favor with God. Behold, you will conceive in your womb and bear a son, and you shall name him Jesus."
–Luke 1:30-31

God sent the Angel Gabriel to Mary, His chosen handmaid, with an incredible message and invitation. Mary said 'Yes,' not only to the conception of the Messiah, but also to all that God willed for her. Mary's 'Yes' perseveres to this day as she continues to allow God to work His perfect Will through her for the salvation of all humanity.

Mary had a vocation, a calling, a role to be fulfilled, from God. I too have a vocation, a particular calling from God that only I can fulfill! If I am called to marriage, God wants me to love my spouse and children generously and selflessly. If I am a priest or religious, God calls me to give myself totally to Him in ministry to others. And on it goes. Let us thank God for the times we have said 'Yes' and ask Him for the grace to respond more like Mary today.

The Visitation
Charity

Elizabeth, filled with the holy Spirit, cried out in a loud voice and said, "Most blessed are you among women, and blessed is the fruit of your womb."
–Luke 1:41-42

When Mary learned of Elizabeth's pregnancy, she went in haste to visit her, to help her, and to encourage her. Mary forgot her own troubles in order to help another. The Lord in turn confirmed to Mary through Elizabeth that "what was spoken to you by the Lord would be fulfilled" (Luke 1:45).

Mary thus teaches us that even in the womb Jesus came not to be served, but to serve. This mystery also proves forever that life begins at conception, since in the womb the unborn John recognized his newly conceived cousin Jesus!

Mary and Elizabeth genuinely cared for one another. Do I put my family and friends in first place? Do I take a sincere interest in them? Mary teaches us to reach out with a heartfelt and sincere love to care for each person who comes into our lives.

The Birth of Jesus
Love of God

The time came for her to have her child, and she gave birth to her firstborn son. She wrapped him in swaddling clothes and laid him in a manger, because there was no room for them in the inn. –Luke 2:6-7

After nine months of waiting and three days of journeying, Joseph and Mary finally found shelter in a little cave carved out of the Bethlehem hills. On this holy night the Son of God came quietly into the world to reclaim it for His Father. He came as a child so no one would refuse Him. He came in poverty so no one would feel inferior. He came defenseless so no one would feel threatened.

That night in Bethlehem, Mary and Joseph needed help. How do I respond when someone asks me for help? Am I willing to "go the extra mile?" Mary and Joseph allowed Jesus to come to us. God now awaits our 'Yes' to allow Him to come to others. May we share His child-like love, His gracious joy, and His gentle care with all we meet, remembering that were Christ to be born in a thousand stables, it would be of no avail, if He were not born in our heart.

The Presentation of Jesus in the Temple
Obedience

When the days were completed for their purification according to the law of Moses, they took him up to Jerusalem to present him to the Lord.
–Luke 2:22

In obedience to the Law of Moses, Mary and Joseph presented Jesus to God in the temple. Israel's long wait for the Messiah was ended. So too was the waiting of old Simeon, who blessed the child and His parents, having been promised by the Spirit that he should not die until he had seen the Lord's Anointed One.

Simeon prayed, "Now, Master, you may let your servant go / in peace, according to your word, / for my eyes have seen your salvation ..." (Luke 2:29-30). Anna, a faithful widow, had also prayed and fasted much for this day, and she rejoiced in it.

As faithful Jews, Mary and Joseph obeyed the Law of God. Am I willing to obey God, to follow His Commandments in Scripture and in the teaching of the Church, even when it takes great courage?

The Finding in the Temple
Zeal

After three days they found him in the temple, sitting in the midst of the teachers, listening to them and asking them questions.
–Luke 2:46

On the way home from the Passover Feast in Jerusalem when Jesus was 12 years old, Mary and Joseph discovered that Jesus was no longer with them. Distraught and frightened, they began looking for Him everywhere. As the hours turned into days, their anxiety grew. Then, after three days, they found Jesus in the Temple! You can imagine their mixed feelings of relief, joy, and even anger.

We too endure times of suffering when it seems we have lost Jesus. As our anxiety grows, we cry out, "Where are you, Lord?" This fifth Joyful Mystery teaches us that God is always in control, and that in time, if we keep looking, we will find Jesus. As His Word declares, "At dusk weeping comes for the night; / but at dawn there is rejoicing" (Psalm 30:6). Mary will lead the way.

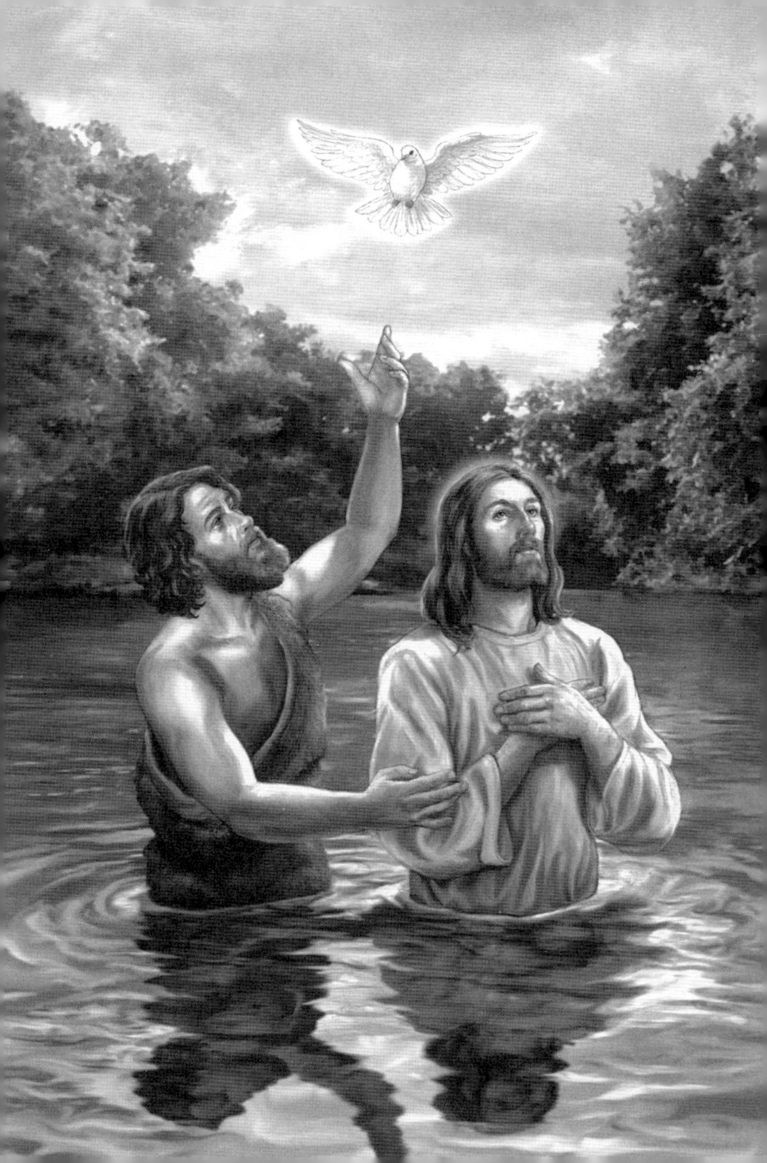

The Luminous Mysteries

The Baptism of Jesus
Obedience

*Then Jesus came from Galilee to John at the Jordan
to be baptized by him.*
–Matthew 3:13

The day was hot; the Baptizer was busy. He looked up to see someone calmly yet resolutely moving down the bank toward him. In a sudden recognition of the Holy One of God, John drew back: "I need to be baptized by you, and yet you are coming to me?" Jesus directed John to allow it, to fulfill all righteousness. After Jesus was baptized, the heavens opened and a voice was heard proclaiming, "This is My beloved Son, with whom I am well pleased."

Jesus had a mission. He accepted his mission, and received the power of the Spirit to carry it out. In addition, he received His Father's affirmation. Each of us has a mission as well, a unique vocation that only we can fulfill, as did Mary, Joseph, John the Baptist and so many others. Today let us seek God's perfect Will for us, and ask Him for the grace to live it out. May His Kingdom come!

The Wedding Feast at Cana
Trust in God

When the wine ran short, the mother of Jesus said to him, "They have no wine." [And] Jesus said to her, "Woman, how does your concern affect me? My hour has not yet come." His mother said to the servers, "Do whatever he tells you."
–John 2:3-5

Mary was concerned for the hosts and guests at the Wedding of Cana, and Jesus allowed her to exercise her gift of intercession. In changing the water into enough wine for several weddings, Jesus displayed God's abundant generosity and opened the hearts of His disciples to faith.

'Saving face' is important in every culture. We want to be at our best and most hospitable when we are entertaining our guests. Sometimes we run out of what we need, and we are helpless. It is then that oftentimes God shows us His unconditional mercy by providing what we need just in time. Let us thank God for this gift and His surprising ways of demonstrating His love for us.

The Proclamation of the Kingdom
Conversion

After John had been arrested, Jesus came to Galilee proclaiming the gospel of God: "This is the time of fulfillment. The kingdom of God is at hand. Repent, and believe in the gospel." –Mark 1:14-15

Jesus preached in the synagogues, streets and hills of Galilee, offering individuals the fulfillment of all their hopes and dreams. People listened, spellbound, as He told them how to gain entrance into this new kingdom: "Repent, turn around, and believe the Good news. God has made a way for you to come back to Him!"

In our universal search for happiness, we have perhaps tried many things—some of which have left us in bondage, unable to break out of the prison that sin has created. Jesus knocks on our door, offering us the remedy. But we must do something—we must repent and believe, that He is the answer, the One who will lead us to true and complete freedom!

The Transfiguration of Jesus
Spirit of Worship

Jesus took Peter, James, and John and led them up a high mountain apart by themselves. And he was transfigured before them, and his clothes became dazzling white, such as no fuller on earth could bleach them. Then Elijah appeared to them along with Moses, and they were conversing with Jesus. –Mark 9:2-4

The disciples climbed a high mountain with Jesus. As the cool Galilean winds blew around them, they saw Jesus growing brighter and brighter until he was literally glowing from within. Suddenly Moses and Elijah appeared, talking with him. The disciples felt they were at heaven's door.

How has God revealed Himself to me? More importantly, how has that encounter changed me? Most of our life is ordinary, yet God is transforming us daily from glory to glory, through the power of His Holy Spirit. Am I open to Him working in me?

The Institution of the Eucharist
Heart of Thanksgiving

While they were eating, he took bread, said the blessing, broke it, and gave it to them, and said, "Take it; this is my body." Then he took a cup, gave thanks, and gave it to them, and they all drank from it.
—Mark 14:22-23

The apostles had enjoyed the unimaginable privilege of living day to day for three years with the Son of the living God! Now, at their most solemn and ancient feast, Jesus suddenly changed the ritual. He proclaimed that the bread and wine were now His body and blood, given for the salvation of all, so that He could be with us forever.

Jesus left us His Body and Blood as both sacrifice and meal. How often do I receive this precious gift? Do I ever consider that God knows exactly what I need to live a truly happy and holy life—and that's why He gave us His Son's body and blood? Let us thank God again for liberating us from the slavery of sin and death and transforming us through the grace of the Eucharist into the image of His Son.

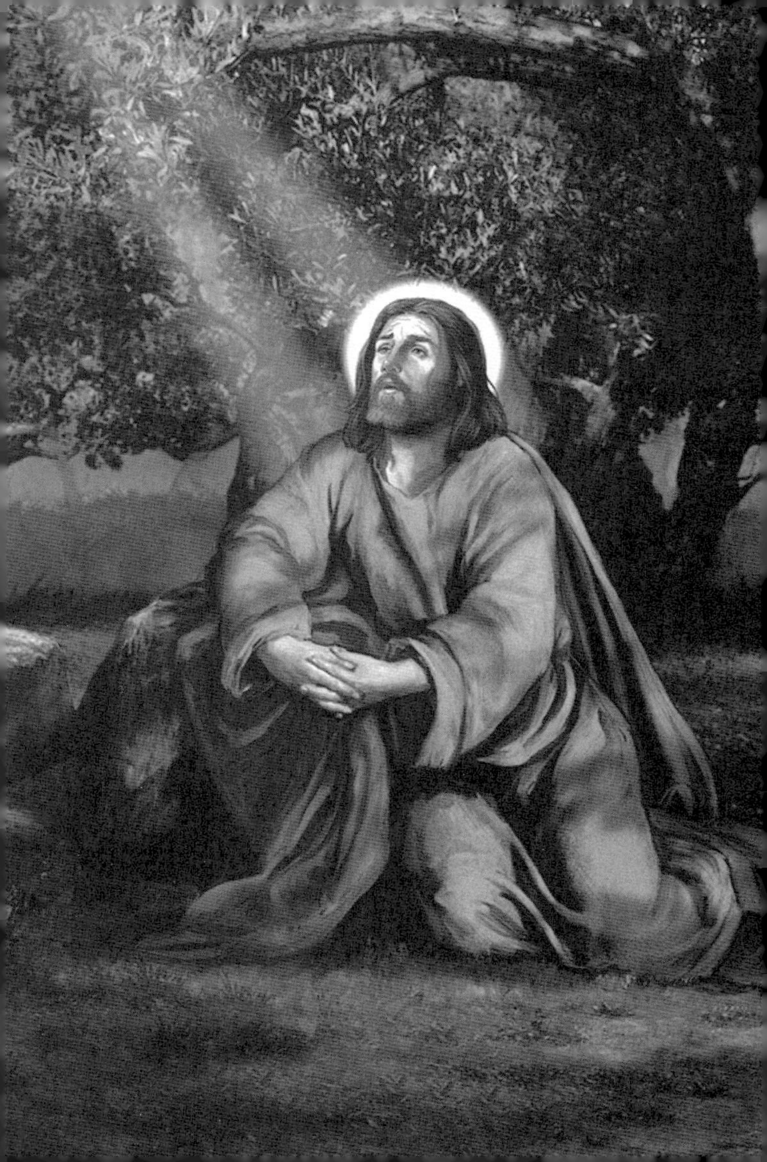

The Sorrowful Mysteries

The Agony in the Garden
Sorrow for Sins

Then they came to a place named Gethsemane, and he said to his disciples, "Sit here while I pray." He took with him Peter, James, and John, and began to be troubled and distressed.
–Mark 14:32-33

As His closest friends slept, Jesus endured alone the extreme agony, fear, and distress of this night of sorrow. Desiring to be spared such great suffering, Jesus prayed, "Abba, Father, all things are possible to you. Take this cup away from me, but not what I will but what you will" (Mark 14:36).

Jesus poured out His anguished heart, begging for the strength to endure the Passion. He placed His full trust and confidence in His Father, as He had done throughout His whole life. And in His Father's embrace Jesus found the strength to go on to the end.

Each of us bears affliction in our own lives and we know many who suffer physically, emotionally, or spiritually. When we are betrayed, abandoned, taken for granted, or suffer illness, or discouragement, let us turn to Jesus for consolation and strength.

The Scourging at the Pillar
Self-Denial

So Pilate, wishing to satisfy the crowd, released Barabbas to them and ... had Jesus scourged.
—Mark 15:15

After being betrayed, falsely accused, and wrongfully imprisoned, Jesus was brought before Pilate for sentencing. His first punishment was a merciless scourging from the Roman soldiers. In his scourging, Jesus was thinking of you. He offered all his suffering to his Father to save us from a punishment we could not bear, fulfilling the words of the Prophet Isaiah: "Upon him was the chastisement that makes us whole, / by his stripes we were healed" (Isaiah 53:5).

Jesus suffered intense, unbearable pain in his scourging. How do I respond to pain? Do I complain or give in to self-pity at the first sign of difficulty? Or do I seek to bear suffering bravely, joining all my sufferings to those of Christ as a living sacrifice for the sake of others, especially His Body on earth and in Purgatory?

Jesus is Crowned with Thorns
Moral Courage

The soldiers... clothed him in purple and, weaving a crown of thorns, placed it on him.
–Mark 15:16-17

The rough Roman soldiers gathered an audience of 600 companions, stripped Jesus of His blood-soaked clothing, and threw a scarlet military cloak over His shoulders. Then they wove a crown of spiked thorns and pressed it down on His head, striking Him and saying, "All hail, King of the Jews!" Jesus courageously and silently endured this piercing public humiliation, choosing to love and forgive His aggressors.

Humiliation is difficult to endure, especially when we are 'in the right.' Jesus lived what He taught about the last being first. When we are treated unfairly, we need to discern the prudent response. Sometimes we need to set our boundaries and stand for what is right; other times we need to 'turn the other cheek' and suffer in silence. In all times we need to follow the counsel of Saint Peter: "Cast all your worries upon him because he cares for you" (1 Peter 5:7).

Jesus Carries the Cross
Patience

So they took Jesus, and carrying the cross himself he went out to what is called the Place of the Skull, in Hebrew, Golgotha.
–John 19:16-17

In total surrender to His Father's Will, Jesus freely accepted the cross and bore it Himself through Jerusalem's narrow and strident streets. Panic attacked him as He struggled to find His footing and fell amidst the shouting and jostling crowd. In their faces He saw hate, rage, and disgust. Saddened but resolute, Jesus kept going, toward His final end.

Sometimes it seems our cross is unbearable, and we panic, thinking we will never be able to complete the course. This fourth Sorrowful Mystery teaches us that God will never allow us to be tested beyond our ability to endure. He will always make a way. As Jesus fell under the agonizing weight of the cross, His Father sent Simon of Cyrene to help Him carry it.

Jesus Dies on the Cross
Final Perseverance

Then they crucified him and divided his garments by casting lots for them to see what each should take.
−Mark 15:24

And so it ended. After a brief life of 33 years, Jesus was betrayed, arrested, tried, convicted, imprisoned, condemned, scourged, crowned with thorns, forced to carry his cross, stripped, nailed, and hung to die, all within 24 hours.

The Good Shepherd went to this extent to rescue His lost sheep, to reopen the gates of heaven and give to us all a second chance at Paradise. Jesus thirsts for us to be with Him, reunited with His Father in the Kingdom for all eternity.

For God so loved the world that he gave his only Son, so that everyone who believes in him might not perish but might have eternal life. − John 3:16

Jesus teaches us through His obedience on the cross to always please the Father. We too will die someday, and prayerful reflection on this fifth Sorrowful Mystery can help prepare us for our own passing. We pray that, at the hour of our death, Mary will be at our side as she was with Jesus, to bring us home with Him.

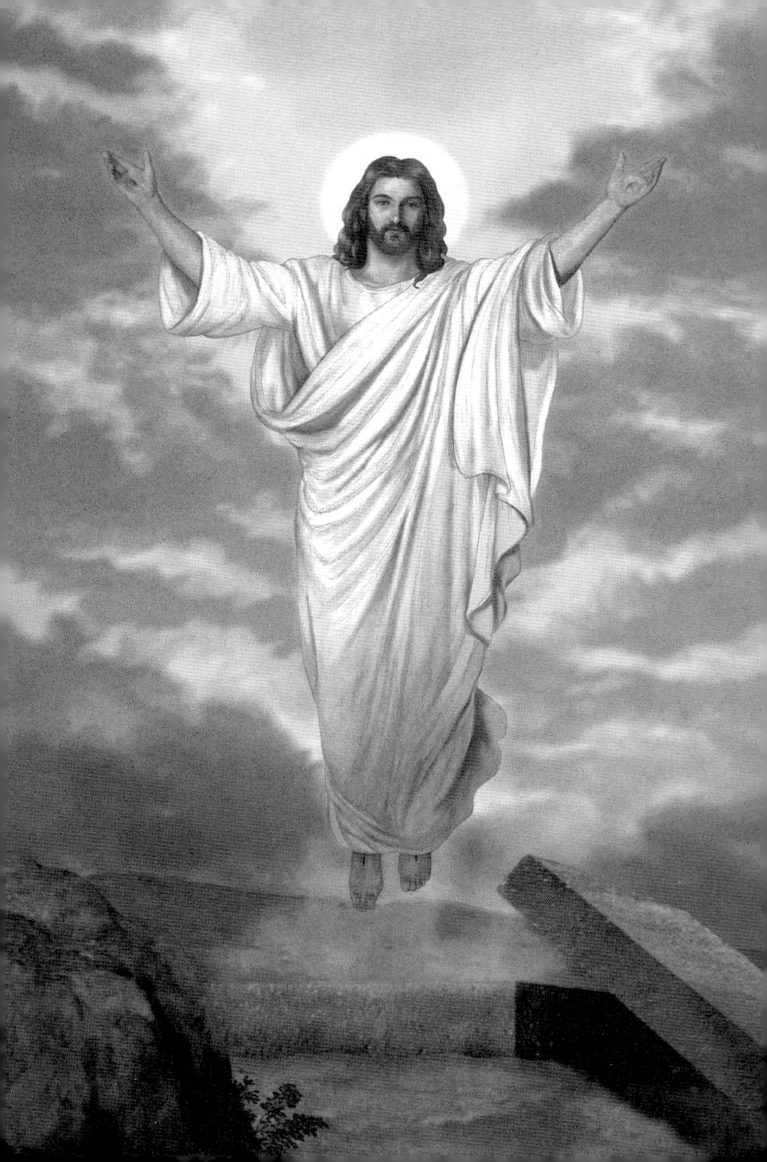

The Glorious Mysteries

The Resurrection of Jesus
Faith

*"Do not be amazed! You seek Jesus of Nazareth, the crucified.
He has been raised; he is not here.
Behold the place where they laid him."*
–Mark 16:6

Somewhere in the night, the Crucified One stepped out of the empty grave with the fire of victory in His heart and an unconquerable joy in His soul as He definitively triumphed over sin and death. Jesus told Mary Magdalene, "Go to my brothers and tell them, 'I am going to my Father and your Father, to my God and your God'" (John 20:17).

Although the Scriptures do not tell us, surely the first person Jesus visited after His Resurrection was His mother. Mary was with Jesus during His birth, His life, and His death. Certainly Jesus would be with Mary at His Resurrection! He is also with us, now and at the hour of our death, preparing a place for us, where we hope to go and be with Him forever.

But there's more. Jesus has given us His Resurrection life so that we might be His presence in our home and in the marketplace. He's alive!

The Ascension of Jesus
Hope

*As he blessed them he parted from them
and was taken up to heaven.*
–Luke 24:51

After His glorious Resurrection, Jesus encouraged His disciples and built up their faith, presenting Himself alive to them by many proofs, appearing and speaking about the kingdom of God. His final blessing gave His disciples peace, favor, strength, and grace to carry out the mission and vision of the Kingdom. They were reminded of Jesus' words: "And if I go and prepare a place for you, I will come back again and take you to myself, so that where I am you also may be" (John 14:3).

Jesus has gone home to His Father. However, He is present to us in His Church, in His Spirit, in His Word, and in His Sacraments, especially the Eucharist; and in many other ways. Do I seek Jesus' presence as I go about my daily life? Do I live now so as to someday join Him in heaven with the Father? Do I set my mind on the things that are above, where Christ is, seated at His Father's right hand?

The Descent of the Holy Spirit
Gifts of the Holy Spirit

*And they were all filled with the holy Spirit and began to speak in different tongues,
as the Spirit enabled them to proclaim.*
–Acts 2:4

After the Ascension, Mary and the disciples were praying together in one place, as Jesus had instructed them. Early Pentecost morning, there came a noise like a strong driving wind that filled the whole house. Tongues as of fire appeared, parted, and rested on each of them. All were filled with the Holy Spirit. Now they could go forth in power, for the Comforter had come!

We too have received the Holy Spirit, in our Baptism and Confirmation, yet there is more. Every morning we can ask the Spirit to fill us anew, and to release in us all of His wonderful gifts. As we live under the anointing of the Holy Spirit, He will produce in us the fruits of love, joy, peace, patience, kindness, generosity, faithfulness, gentleness, and self-control. He will give us the New Wine!

The Assumption of Mary
A Happy Death

If we have died with him we shall also live with him;
if we persevere we shall also reign with him.
−2 Timothy 2:11-12

The Church teaches that Mary, the Mother of Jesus, was taken up body and soul into heaven after the completion of her earthly life. Because of her Immaculate Conception, Mary was freed from the consequences of Original Sin. Mary is both a sign of what heaven holds for us and also a Mother to help us get there. In the words of Saint Paul, "Just as we have borne the image of the earthly one, we shall also bear the image of the heavenly one" (1 Corinthians 15:49).

Mary had a calling, as does each of us. In the beginning we make our choices, and in the end, our choices make us. Am I ready to meet the Lord now? Do I pray for the grace of a happy death? Now is the time to wake from sleep and prepare for the hour of death. Mary will help us experience the glorious truth that "Death is swallowed up in victory" (1 Corinthians 15:54).

The Coronation of Mary
Love of Mary

*A great sign appeared in the sky, a woman clothed with the
sun, with the moon under her feet,
and on her head a crown of twelve stars.*
–Revelation 12:1

The Rosary begins with Isaiah's sign: *The virgin shall be with child, and bear a son*, and ends by encouraging us to look to Mary, the woman clothed with the sun. Mary is not only Mother, but also Queen of the Universe, reigning now with her Son, rewarded by God for being His most faithful disciple.

Mary's mission endures until the end of time, to mother all of us, her children, through our lives on earth and into the heavenly kingdom, our true home. As Saint Therese of Lisieux said, "Mary is more Mother than Queen." In this mystery let us consider our relationship with Mary. The Church encourages us to consecrate ourselves to her and to ask her help in doing whatever Jesus tells us.

"And he will reign forever and ever."
– Revelation 11:15

The Rosary and the Battle of Lepanto
Our Lady of the Rosary

As believers, our primary struggle is with spiritual principalities and powers, yet sometimes we do fight physical enemies, and history records a number of mighty victories attributed to the Rosary. Of all these, perhaps the most striking is the Battle of Lepanto.

In the 16th century, the Moslem Turks amassed a huge naval fleet and set sail to attack Europe at the Bay of Lepanto, Italy. Pope Saint Pius V called for a crusade among Europe's Christian nations and appointed a leader. He ordered the 40 Hours Devotion to be held in Rome, and urged everyone to pray the Rosary. Every man in the small Christian armada received the sacraments and prayed the Rosary before engaging the enemy.

On Sunday morning, October 7, 1565, the Christian fleet sailed out to meet the undefeated Turks, while all Europe prayed. After a day of bitter fighting and miraculous intervention, the Christians vanquished the Turks, who fled in disarray. Pope Pius V commemorated October 7th in honor of Our Lady of Victory, and in 1573 Pope Gregory XIII proclaimed the date as the Feast of the Holy Rosary.

The Rosary Novena

After Jesus ascended into heaven, Mary and the disciples prayed for nine days—the first novena. On the 10th day, the feast of Pentecost, God sent His promised Holy Spirit, and the Church was born.

The novena, then, is a traditional Catholic way of praying with perseverance, as Jesus has commanded. The Rosary Novena originated in 1884, when Our Blessed Mother appeared at the Sanctuary of Our Lady of the Rosary of Pompeii at Naples, saying, "Whoever desires to obtain favors from me should make three novenas of the Rosary in petition, and three novenas in thanksgiving."

Pray five decades of the Rosary daily for 27 days in petition for a favor, and 27 days in thanksgiving. On the first day, pray the Joyful Mysteries; on the second, pray the Luminous Mysteries; on the third, the Sorrowful Mysteries; on the fourth day, pray the Glorious Mysteries, and so forth throughout the 54 days.

Novenas of Petition									Novenas of Thanksgiving								
1 J	2 L	3 S	4 G	5 J	6 L	7 S	8 G	9 J	1 J	2 L	3 S	4 G	5 J	6 L	7 S	8 G	9 J
10 L	11 S	12 G	13 J	14 L	15 S	16 G	17 J	18 L	10 L	11 S	12 G	13 J	14 L	15 S	16 G	17 J	18 L
19 S	20 G	21 J	22 L	23 S	24 G	25 J	26 L	27 S	19 S	20 G	21 J	22 L	23 S	24 G	25 J	26 L	27 S

The History of Apparitions in the Catholic Church

The Holy Scriptures record many heavenly visions and apparitions given to us humans for the purposes of God, the Creator of all. In the New Testament, Moses and Elijah appeared to and spoke with Jesus in His Transfiguration. Jesus Himself appeared to His Apostles and other disciples after His Resurrection.

In fact, Scripture records that "tombs were opened, and the bodies of many saints who had fallen asleep were raised. And coming forth from their tombs after his resurrection, they entered the holy city and appeared to many" (Matthew 27:52-53).

On the road to Damascus, Saint Paul had a heavenly vision that changed not only the course of his travels but of history as well. And so it goes.

In the fourth century, Saint Gregory of Nyssa recorded that Our Blessed Mother had appeared to Saint Gregory the Wonderworker, who died in 270 AD.

The number of reported apparitions reached almost 800 in the 13th century, to such visionaries as Saint Dominic, Saint Francis of Assisi, Saint Rose of Viterbo, Saint Simon Stock (Our Lady of Mount Carmel), and many more. It was truly a century visited with great graces from heaven.

In the 16th century, apparitions moved from being mainly private and personal to more public. It seems that God sent His Mother in these "newer" apparitions to renew faith and help deal with world crises. In 1531, for example, Our Lady of Guadalupe appeared to Saint Juan Diego, sparking a revival that led to the conversion of 9 million Aztecs!

The last 200 years have seen the majority of Church-approved apparitions, beginning in 1830, with the appearance of Our Blessed Mother and the gift of the Miraculous Medal to Saint Catherine Labouré in Paris. Since then, there have been a number of major approved apparitions of Mary.

In all this we see our dear Lord constantly and consistently sending His Mother to warn us in her own inimitable way to reform our lives and return to her Son. Historically we have not taken action as promptly and obediently as we might. How will we respond this time?

> *Therefore, stay awake, for you know*
> *neither the day nor the hour.*
> – Matthew 25:13

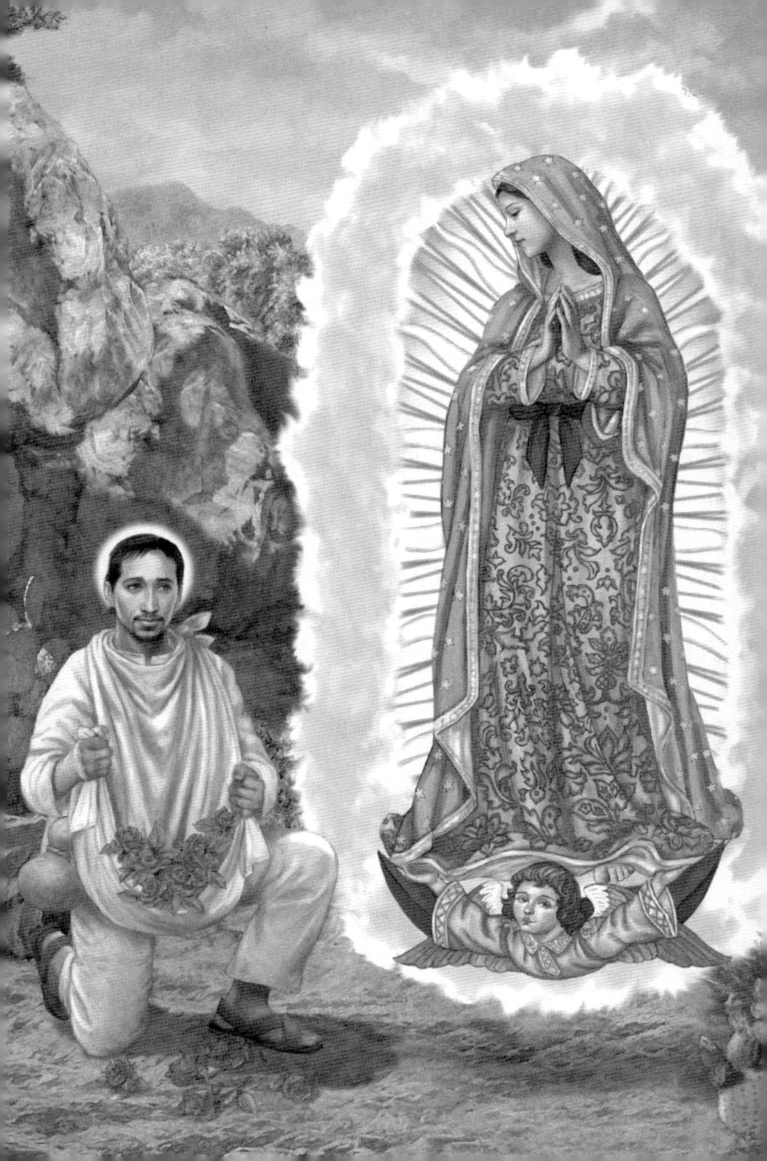

Our Lady of Guadalupe
La Alma de la Gente

In the early 16th century, the Aztec Indians ruled Mexico and much of Central America. Their leader, Montezuma, reigned from an island in Lake Texcoco called Mexico City, home of the people called the Mexica. The Aztecs sacrificed thousands of captives a year to appease their bloodthirsty gods.

On Good Friday, 1519, Hernando Cortez, a Spanish conquistador, landed on the Gulf shore of Mexico with soldiers and horses. After many months, Cortez defeated the Aztecs and stopped their horrific blood-sacrifices. Spanish missionaries tried to teach the Aztecs about Jesus and the Catholic faith, but most of the Indians welcomed neither the missionaries nor their new religion.

One who did believe and was baptized was Juan Diego, whose Aztec name meant "Singing Eagle." A widower, Juan cared for his sick uncle, Juan Bernardino, who was also a Catholic. Juan worked in the fields and wove mats.

On Saturday morning, December 9th, 1531, as was his custom, Juan was running the seven miles from his village to the church for Mass. As he mounted the small hill of Tepeyac, he heard the sweet, shrill song of birds chirping, which ceased as suddenly as it had begun. Juan stopped, amazed. At that moment, from the top of the hill, he heard a young woman's voice calling his name: "Juanito!"

Looking up, Juan saw rays like the sun beaming brightly around the head and feet of what appeared to be a young Aztec princess. She was about 16 years old and so very beautiful! She wore a turquoise-blue cape covered in stars. The woman said, "Juan, smallest and dearest of my little children, where are you going? Dear little son, I love you. I am the ever-Virgin Mary, Mother of the true God who gives life."

The beautiful Lady continued, "God made everything and He is in all places. He is the Lord of heaven and earth. I desire a temple, a church, in this place where I will show my love to your people. I want to show my compassion to all people who ask my help. Here I will see their tears. I will console them and they will be at ease. Run now to tell the bishop all you have seen and heard."

Juan Diego ran as fast as he could to the palace of Bishop Zumarraga in Mexico City. After listening kindly to Juan, the bishop dismissed him, saying he would think about his request. Saddened that the bishop did not believe him, Juan walked slowly home. As he passed the hill of Tepeyac, suddenly the beautiful

Lady appeared to him again. "Listen, my little son," she said. "Tomorrow go to see the bishop again and tell him the Virgin Mary greatly desires for him to build a church in this place."

Sunday morning, Juan saw the bishop, who asked for a sign. Mary said, "Very well, my little son. Come back tomorrow and I will give you a sign." However, Juan's uncle grew more ill, and Juan did not return to the Lady until the morning of December 12th. "My little son," Mary said, "do not be afraid. Am I not here who am your Mother? Are you not under my protection? Your uncle will not die. At this very moment he is cured."

Juan felt a deep peace in his heart. Mary told him to climb Mount Tepeyac and cut the flowers growing there. Knowing that no flowers ever grew in the cold winter, Juan obediently ascended the hill, where he beheld beautiful roses such as only grew in Spain! Juan put them in his tilma, which was like a cape worn in front of him.

Mary arranged the roses tenderly with her own hands, and then tied the tilma in back of Juan so that none of the flowers would drop out. She told him, "Do not let anyone but the bishop see what you are carrying. Tell him everything you have seen and heard this morning. This time he will believe you."

Juan Diego rushed to the bishop, and told him everything that Mary had instructed him to say. Then Juan reached up and untied his tilma. His cloak fell open before the bishop, and the roses tumbled out at his feet. The bishop fell to his knees in amazement, as did his servants. They pointed to Juan's cloak in awe. Juan looked down in front of him. To his wonder he saw the Virgin herself, imprinted on his tilma!

The bishop and his servants spent some time in holy silence and prayer before the image. Then the bishop slowly arose, gently untied the tilma from around Juan's neck, and carried it into his private chapel. The next morning he and his priests carried the tilma of Juan Diego in procession to the cathedral. The news of the miraculous image and message of the Lady spread quickly that morning throughout Mexico City.

Meanwhile, Juan's uncle told Juan that, as he lay dying, a beautiful lady had appeared to him in a gentle glow of light. She told him he would recover from his illness, and that she had sent his nephew with a picture of herself to the Bishop. "Call me and my image Santa Maria of Guadalupe," she said, and then she vanished. "Guadalupe" was the name of a Marian shrine in Spain. However, it also sounded like the Aztec word for "She who crushes the serpent."

The Indians helped Bishop Zumarraga build a

small church on the hill of Tepeyac. The bishop also built a little chapel nearby for Juan Diego. Many people came to see the miracle and to pray before the image of the beautiful Lady.

Juan Diego told his fellow Aztecs and the other Indians the story of Our Lady of Guadalupe and urged them to accept Jesus and the Catholic Faith. The Indians especially were moved by the love of this Mother who looked like them and spoke their language, which included pictures. The image of Our Lady spoke to them in a very special way. She had appeared to one of their own people, an Aztec, on the hill of Tepeyac, which had been the mount of their mother-god.

The Lady stood in front of the sun, with its rays shining behind her. This meant she was greater than the sun-god of the Aztecs. She stood on the moon, which meant she had triumphed over the moon-god. Her cloak was a blue-green, which meant she was a Queen. The stars on her cloak told them she was greater than the stars which they worshipped.

The Lady's hands were folded in prayer and her head was bowed. This told the Aztecs that she was not a god, but was honoring the true God who was greater than her. She wore a tiny black cross on a gold medal around her neck. This meant she was the same religion as the Spanish conquerors. Her rose-colored dress symbolized the sun rising to give new life.

The Lady's face was so very kind and full of compassion. She was standing on the head of a snake, which meant she had crushed the devil. The black band around her waist was a sign that she was pregnant, and was carrying a baby in her womb. It also meant she was offering this baby to them and to all the peoples of the New World. A tiny flower was placed over her womb, a sign of her holy Child.

Juan Diego explained to his listeners that Mary, the Mother of Jesus, was the Mother of the true God. Her religion, the religion of Christianity, was to replace the Aztec religion. He taught the Aztecs that God had sent his only Son to die for all people. His one sacrifice saved them all.

In the next few years, 9 million Indians were baptized! After their conversion, the people learned more about Jesus and Mary and their new-found faith. Many of them married the Spaniards, and the Mexicans came to be a new people.

In 1709, the first basilica of Our Lady of Guadalupe was built, and her image on the tilma was installed above the altar. In 1945, Pope Pius XII proclaimed our Lady of Guadalupe as the Patroness of all the Americas. In 1976, a new basilica, which holds up to 10,000 people, was dedicated. Each year over 10 million people visit the Basilica of Our Lady of Guadalupe, making it the most popular shrine of Our Blessed Mother Mary in the whole world!

Saint John Paul II visited the shrine of the Virgin of Guadalupe in 1979, one year after his election, and again in 1990, when he beatified Juan Diego. In 2002, the Holy Father made his final visit to Mexico, during which he canonized Saint Juan Diego. Saint John Paul honored Juan Diego for his simple faith and trust in God. Juan Diego had told Mary that he was a "small rope or a tiny ladder," but he allowed God to use him to bring Jesus to many, many natives, and Our Lady took her rightful place as "La Alma de la Gente"—"the Soul of the People."

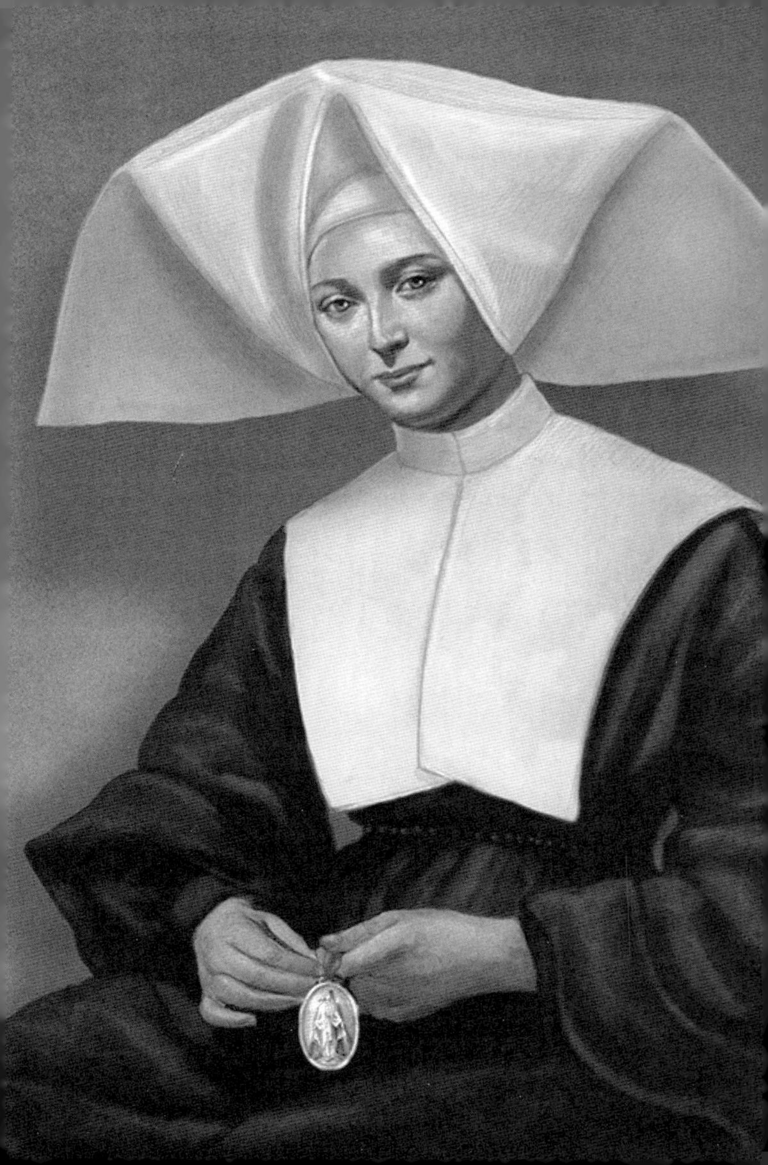

Our Lady of the Miraculous Medal

*A great sign appeared in the sky, a woman clothed with the
sun, with the moon under her feet,
and on her head a crown of twelve stars.*
– Revelation 12:1

Catherine Labouré was born on May 2, 1806, in a small village in Burgundy, France, famous for its meadows and vineyards. Her educated father was a prosperous farmer. Her quiet and gentle mother was a former school teacher who was fully engaged in raising her family of eleven! Even so, Madame Labouré instilled in her ninth child a deep love for God and His ways. Tragically, she died when Catherine was only nine. In her sorrow, little Catherine clasped a statue of the Virgin Mary to her breast and said, "Now, dear Blessed Mother, you will be my mother." And so it came to pass.

Catherine had only a very rudimentary schooling. "From the time of her First Communion at the age of 12," writes her sister Antoinette, "she became entirely mystic." Her father decided to have Catherine run the household, a huge task for such a young lady, as she had an invalid sister as well as 14 hired hands to care for. Nonetheless, Catherine found time to walk six miles before dawn every day to attend Mass in the nearby village.

At the age of 18, Catherine dreamed of an old, venerable priest who began to celebrate Mass, with Catherine in attendance. After Mass, he beckoned her to come towards him, but she backed off, all the while keeping her eyes on him. Catherine left there and went to visit a village invalid. The old priest appeared again, and said to her, "My child, you are doing well to visit the sick. You run from me now, but one day you will be glad to come to me. God has plans for you; don't forget it." Some time later, Catherine visited a hospital of the Daughters of Charity, and on the wall saw a picture of the priest who had been in her dream. His name? Saint Vincent de Paul!

At the age of 24, Catherine entered the Daughters of Charity in Paris. For three days, she saw a vision of the heart of Saint Vincent above his relics. Afterwards, every time Catherine entered the chapel during her nine month's novitiate, she saw a vision of Jesus truly present in the Holy Eucharist.

On the eve of the feast of Saint Vincent de Paul, July 19, 1830, Catherine was awakened by a little child standing before her in a brilliant light. "Sister Labouré," the child said, "come to the Chapel; the Blessed Virgin awaits you." Catherine followed the child—her guardian angel—to the chapel, and after some moments she saw a lady seating herself in a chair on the altar steps.

Catherine threw herself upon Our Blessed Mother, resting her hands upon Mary's lap. Our Lady spoke with Catherine for two hours, and then disappeared.

Our Blessed Mother Mary told Catherine that God had a mission for her. She would have much to suffer, but would rise above the sufferings by God's grace and the knowledge she was serving God. Furthermore, Our Lady foretold the overthrow of the French government, and begged Catherine to pray.

Four months later, on November 27th, 1830, during evening prayers in the chapel, Our Blessed Mother appeared again. Her feet were resting on a globe, and she was standing on a serpent. She had twelve stars about her head. Mary had rings on her fingers, with beautiful gems, from which shone shimmering rays of light. Mary explained that the rays symbolized the graces she shed upon those who asked her for them. She also said the gems from which no rays fell were the graces for which souls forget to ask.

An oval frame then formed around Mary. In letters of gold the following words appeared within the oval: "O Mary, conceived without sin, pray for us who have recourse to thee." Our Lady next showed Catherine the back of the image, which portrayed a large M surmounted by a bar and a cross. Beneath it there appeared the Hearts of Jesus and Mary.

Our Blessed Mother Mary instructed Catherine to make a medal of the image and to spread devotion to her Immaculate Conception. "All who wear this medal will receive great graces; they should wear it around the neck. Graces will abound for those who wear it with confidence." Catherine was to tell the vision only to her confessor. Sister Labouré did so, and her confessor saw to it that the medal was made and distributed, all the while keeping Catherine's identity a secret. Only near her death, 45 years later, did Catherine reveal her secret to her superior.

In 1832, the first medals were struck, and shortly thereafter hundreds of millions of medals were distributed throughout the world. So many miracles happened to those who wore the medal that it became known simply as the Miraculous Medal.

Sister Catherine Labouré died on December 31, 1876. Because of her heroic practice of the virtues of everyday love of God and selfless humble service of others as a religious, Saint Catherine Labouré was canonized in 1947. Her incorrupt body lies today in a glass coffin in Paris.

Saint Catherine Labouré heralded the "Age of Mary." This first apparition would be joined by others, stretching from La Salette to Banneux to present-day apparitions whose validity remains to be authenticated by Rome. Mary's approach shows that she is concerned with each of us personally. The Miraculous Medal is a link between Mary and the wearer; it is efficacious in helping to promote and deepen our personal devotion to Mary as well as helping us to renew the world.

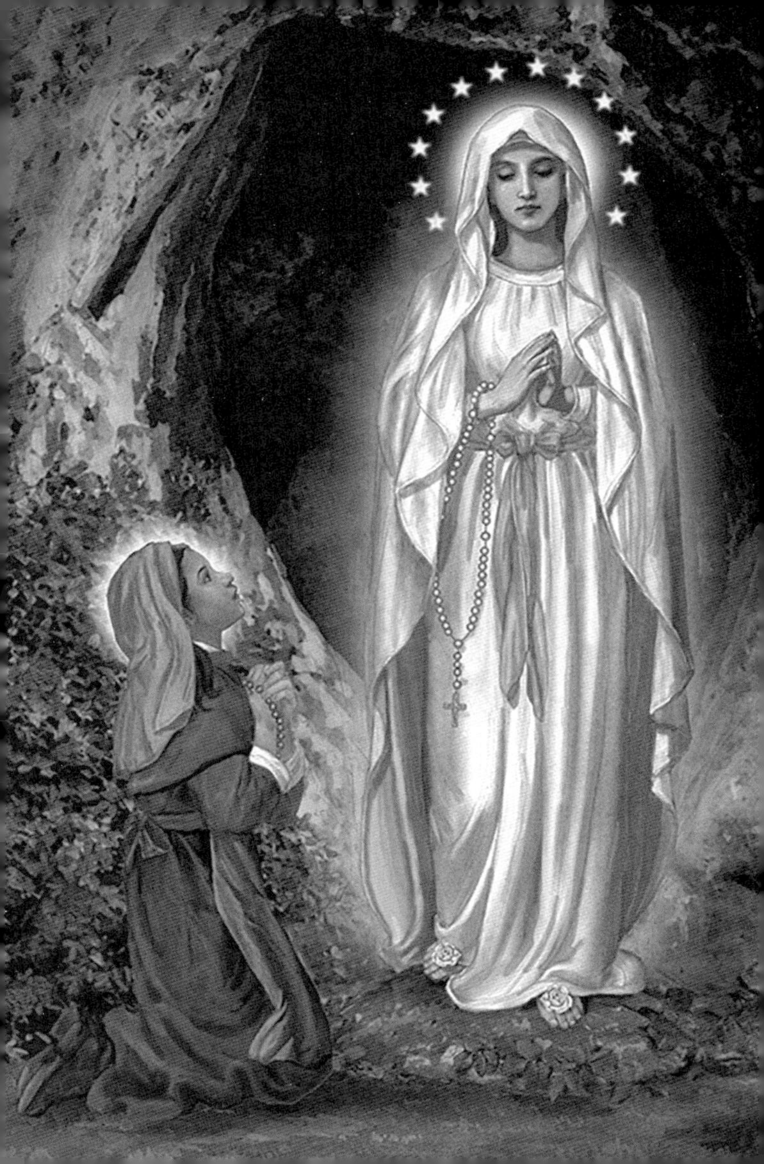

Our Lady of Lourdes

Bernadette Soubirous, a quiet and modest girl with a good sense of humor and an attractive personality was born in 1844 as the eldest child of a poor couple in Lourdes, France. The Soubirous family was at this time living in a small dark cottage known as Le Cachot—a converted jail! Not far from their little home flowed the river Gave.

Thus it was on the 11th of February, 1858, that 14-year old Bernadette went to the river with her sister and a friend to gather firewood. The two girls went ahead and Bernadette found herself alone, across from the grotto of Massabielle. Suddenly she heard the noise of a sudden rush of wind and saw a golden cloud moving out from the cave behind the grotto.

To her amazement, Bernadette saw an "exceedingly beautiful" Lady clothed in a blue and white dress appear above a rose bush. The Lady smiled at Bernadette and made the Sign of the Cross with a golden rosary. Bernadette knelt down and began to pray. The Lady fingered her rosary with Bernadette and smiled, joining her only in praying the Gloria at the end of each decade.

Bernadette told her mother what had happened. Mrs. Soubirous reluctantly allowed Bernadette and her sister to return to the grotto three days later, where Bernadette again saw the beautiful Lady holding a rosary.

The next Thursday, the Lady asked Bernadette to come to the grotto for fifteen days. The Lady said, "I promise you happiness, not in this world but in the next." She continued, "I would like to see many people come here." In her sixth appearance, the Lady said, "Pray much for poor sinners," which Bernadette did from then on.

On February 25th, the Lady told Bernadette, "Drink from the fountain and bathe in it." Obediently Bernadette scratched in the gravel and soon a little pool of water formed, from which Bernadette drank and washed her face. In two days the pool became a stream. Within two weeks a blind man was healed and a dying child miraculously restored to health!

The Lady instructed Bernadette to tell the clergy to build a chapel on the site of the grotto, and that people should walk there in procession. Bernadette related these commands to her pastor, who curtly directed Bernadette to ask the Lady her name.

Thus it was on the feast of the Annunciation, March 25th, 1858, that the Lady told Bernadette, "I am the Immaculate Conception." Bernadette repeated the Lady's name to the stunned priest, who responded,

"Can you ever forgive me for doubting your visions of the Mother of God?"

Bernadette saw Our Lady two more times, and then, like the rest of us, lived the remainder of her life by faith, not by sight. She joined the Sisters of Charity in Nevers, France, and died there in 1879 at the young age of 35 from incurable tuberculosis.

Each year more than five million pilgrims travel to the grotto of Massabielle in Lourdes, the most famous modern shrine of Our Lady, to honor and ask the intercession of Mary, the Mother of Jesus, and to seek healing of spirit, soul, and body. The water from the spring continues to show remarkable healing power to this day, bringing medically documented healings to many people. Pope Pius XI canonized Saint Bernadette in 1933, and her body remains entirely and miraculously incorrupt at her convent in France.

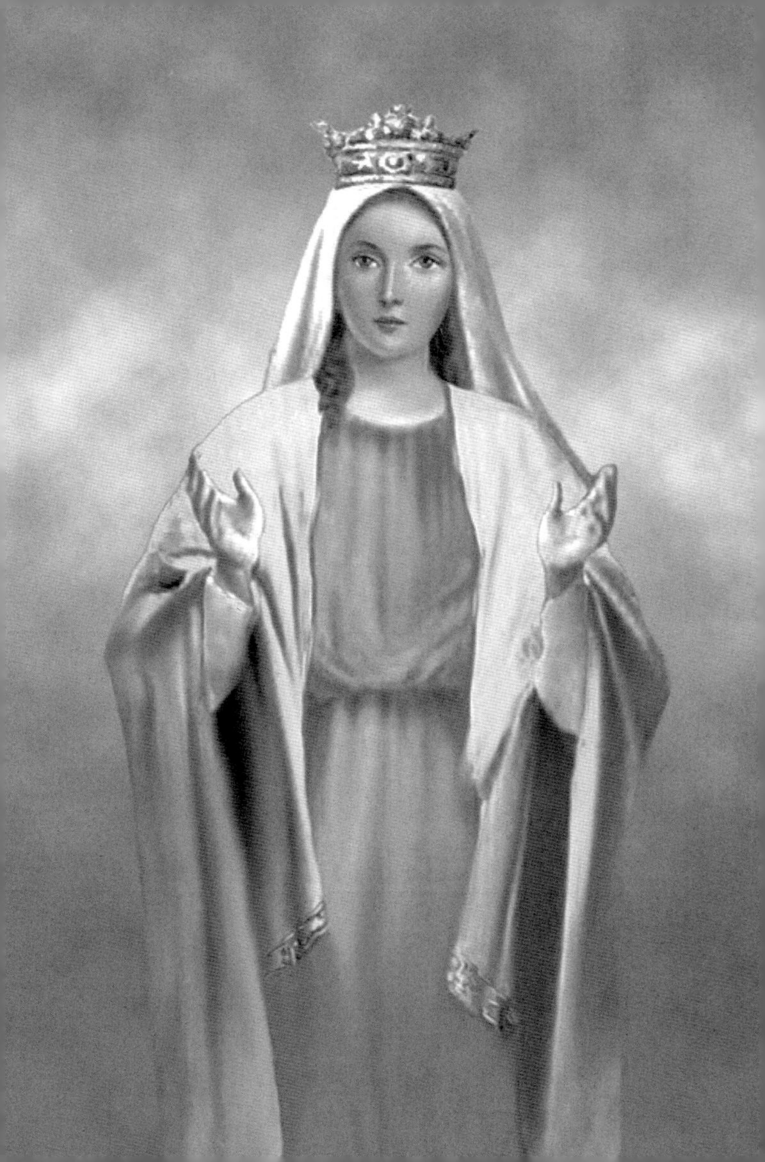

Our Lady of Knock
Queen of Ireland

Saint Patrick preached the Good News of Jesus and converted the Emerald Isle to the Catholic faith in the first half of the fifth century. He had a great devotion to Mary, the Mother of God, and built a great abbey church in her honor. Over the years, the Irish suffered greatly for their devotion to the Faith and the Blessed Mother, yet they clung to their Catholicism tenaciously.

Thus it was that Father Bartholomew Cavanagh, a saintly priest with a deep and fervent devotion to the Mother of God and the Holy Souls in Purgatory, came to be appointed in 1867 as pastor of the little church of Saint John the Baptist in Knock, County Mayo. Popular tradition holds that Saint Patrick stopped at Knock, blessed it, and prophesied that one day it would become a center of devotion, attracting many pilgrims.

Life was very difficult in Ireland, as greedy landlords exacted high rents, evicting many villagers from their homes and forcing them to emigrate. Famines and fevers alike combined to lay difficult burdens on the remaining families.

In 1879, Father Cavanagh offered 100 consecutive Masses for the Holy Souls in Purgatory. The final Mass was celebrated on Thursday, August 21st, the vigil—at that time—of the Assumption of Mary into heaven. That afternoon, stormy rain clouds rumbled across the sky, and by 7 PM a steady downpour ensued. Mary McLoughlin, the rectory housekeeper, was returning home with her friend, Mary Byrne, when the two women beheld a brilliant light shining on the south gable wall of the church. In the midst of the light the two Marys perceived three figures, whom they excitedly identified as Our Lady, Saint Joseph, and Saint John the Evangelist!

In a short time, 18 villagers, aged 5 to 75, were gathered at the gable wall. The witnesses themselves later described the light as a sparkling, almost pulsating light that made the rainy night sky appear brighter than noonday and the gable wall itself as white as snow.

Pilgrims to Knock discovered that healings began to occur when they drank water mixed with a bit of cement from the gable wall. Amidst mounting evidence, an Ecclesiastical Commission ruled in October, 1879, that the testimony of the original witnesses was trustworthy and satisfactory, and confirmed this with another investigation in 1936.

Over the last century, multitudes of documented healings have been reported by pilgrims traveling to Knock from all over the world. Father Cavanagh, who did not see the apparitions, nonetheless believed them and served all who came to the apparition site until his death on December 8th, 1897—the feast of the Immaculate Conception. Monsignor James Horan, pastor of Knock from 1967 until 1986, oversaw the building of the Knock Basilica just in time for the visit of Saint John Paul II to the shrine in 1979.

The very silence of the apparition at Knock has invited the faithful to contemplate that the villagers who witnessed it, and, by extension, all Catholics, were present at a heavenly liturgy, with Our Blessed Mother and Saint Joseph leading us in silent prayer as Saint John preached and Jesus, the Lamb of God, stood silently on the altar. Many assert that Our Lady is interceding for us, and particularly the people of Ireland, that we should not lose faith but continue ever more fervently to worship God and receive the Eucharist, our true and eternal Bread of Life.

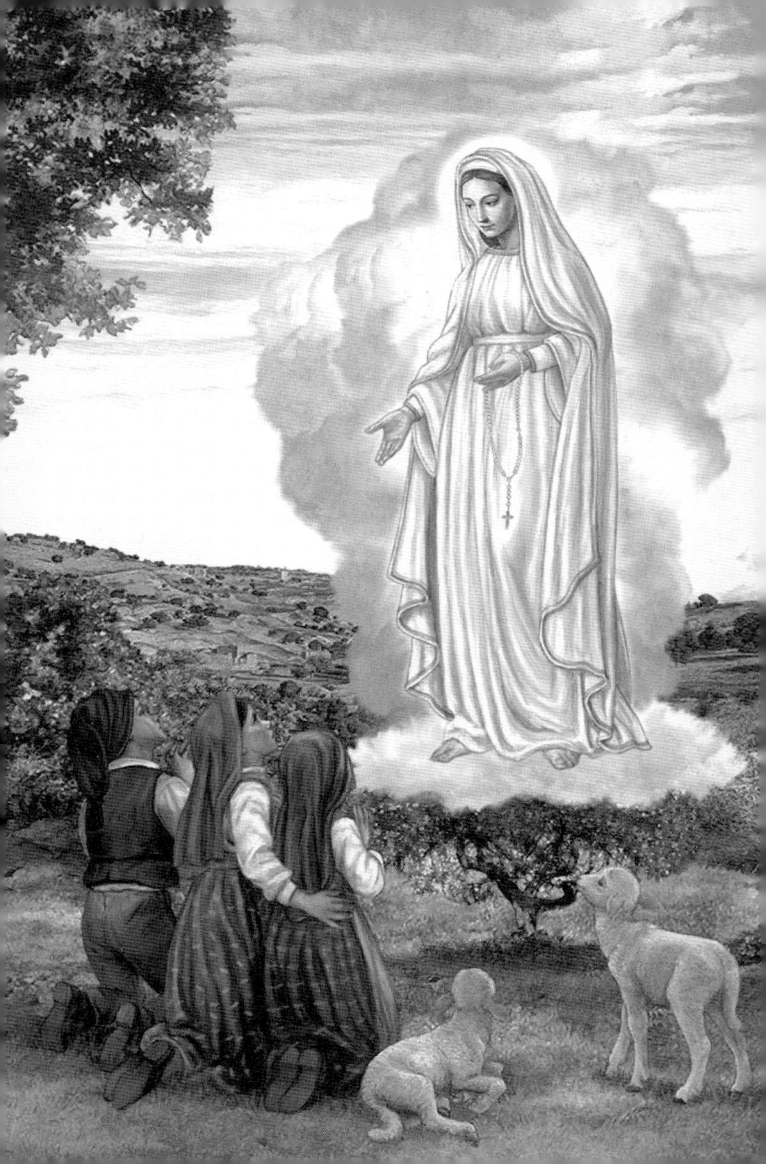

Our Lady of Fatima
Queen of Peace

As we have seen, Our Blessed Mother has visited our earth at key times in the lives of her children, as the challenges and difficulties of our civilization increase. Such was the case in Portugal a century ago. In 1910, the Portuguese monarchy was disbanded in favor of an anticlerical republic which put most Church properties under state control.

Even so, the majority of the Portuguese were Roman Catholic, practicing the ancient Faith which actually predated the founding of their country. Portuguese villagers, such as those in the diocese of Leiria and the rural villages of Aljustrel and Fatima, especially loved our Blessed Mother, and faithfully prayed her Rosary.

In the spring of 1916, World War I, which would eventually claim 17 million lives, was raging across Europe, while in faraway Moscow, Vladimir Lenin was laying the groundwork for the Communist Revolution.

In the little village of Fatima, 9- year-old Lucia dos Santos and her cousins, 7-year-old Francisco and 5-year-old Jacinta Marto, were tending their sheep one day when they heard a strong wind in the trees and saw brilliant rays of light, which formed into the shape of a luminous young man. He said, "Fear not. I am the Angel of peace. Pray with me." Kneeling and bowing low, he prayed three times, "My God, I believe, I adore, I hope, and I love You. I ask pardon of all those who do not believe, do not adore, do not hope, and do not love You." Then he said, "The Hearts of Jesus and Mary are attentive to the voice of your supplication."

Lucia later wrote of this moment, "We felt the presence of God so intensely, so intimately, that we dared not speak even to one another. The next day we felt ourselves still enveloped by its atmosphere." This deep sense of God's anointing remained with the children for quite some time. They would attend morning Mass and then set out to find the best grazing they could on the rather sparse hills.

One day, a few months later, the Angel again appeared to the children, saying, "What are you doing? Pray, pray a great deal. The Hearts of Jesus and Mary have designs of mercy for you. Offer unceasingly to the Most High prayer and sacrifices."

The Angel said, "Offer up everything within your power as a sacrifice to the Lord in reparation for the sins by which He is offended, and in supplication for sinners. In this way you will bring peace to our country, for I am the Guardian Angel of Portugal. Above all, bear and accept with patience the sufferings that God may send you."

Lucia and Jacinta could hear the Angel, while Francisco could only see him. Nonetheless, when the girls told him the Angel's words, they sank deeply into his soul, as he said, "like a gleaming torch, showing us who God is, what is His love for us, and how he wants us to love Him too; the value of sacrifice and how it pleases Him; how He receives it for the conversion of sinners. That is why from that moment we began to offer Him whatever mortified us."

The Angel of Portugal appeared once more in the autumn of 1916. He knelt before a chalice suspended in the air, over which was a Host dripping blood into the chalice. After teaching the children a prayer, he gave them each Holy Communion, again asking reparation for the sins of men.

On May 13, 1917, a tremendous light flashed in the sky over the Cova de Iria, where the children were tending their sheep. Lucia writes that out of the light stepped "the most beautiful Lady" she had ever seen. "It was a Lady dressed all in white, more brilliant than the sun, shedding rays of light clearer and stronger than a crystal glass filled with the most sparkling water and pierced by the burning rays of the sun." The Lady was about 16 years old, tenderly solicitous, yet with a certain sadness in her eyes. Her delicate, slender hands were folded in prayer, holding a luminous white rosary.

"I come from Heaven," the Lady said. She asked the children to return on the 13th of each month and promised in October to tell them who she was and what she wanted of them. She asked the children if they would offer themselves to God and accept any suffering He wished to send them, in reparation for sin and the conversion of sinners. The children acquiesced, and the Lady replied, "Then you will suffer much, but God's grace will strengthen you."

With each visit, Our Blessed Mother gave messages to the children, revealing that she would take Francisco and Jacinta to heaven in a short while, but that Lucia would remain to establish devotion to Mary's Immaculate Heart.

Mary explained that war was a punishment for sin, and if people continued to disobey God's Will, they would suffer consequences of war, hunger, and persecution of the Church. She also prophesied that Russia would "spread her errors" of atheism and materialism across the earth.

Our Lady of Fatima repeatedly emphasized the necessity of praying daily, especially the Rosary, of wearing the Brown Scapular, and of performing acts of reparation and sacrifice. She also promised a sign as proof of her messages, and prophesied that if people did not heed her warnings, a new and more terrible war would come. She asked that Russia be consecrated to her Immaculate Heart, and that Catholics offer their Holy Communions on the first Saturday of each month in reparation for sin. Mary promised that in the end, her Immaculate Heart would triumph, and the world would enjoy an era of peace.

On the stormy night of October 12th, 1917, thousands of people made their way to the tiny hamlet of Fatima for the promised miracle. October 13th dawned cold and rainy as Mr. Marto led Lucia, Francisco, and Jacinta to the Cova. A few moments past noon there came the familiar flash of light, and Our Blessed Mother appeared again to the children.

Mary identified herself as the Lady of the Rosary. Her last words to the children were: "People must amend their lives, ask pardon for their sins, and not offend Our Lord any more, for He is already too greatly offended." As she departed, Mary opened her hands, and rays of bright light extended from them to the sun.

Seventy thousand people—believers, clergy, journalists, officials, and scoffers—suddenly saw the sun twist into a silver disc, shooting off multi-colored light rays in every direction. The careening sun spun madly on its axis and then hurtled down toward the terrified crowd. Amid the people's prayers and cries, the dancing disc abruptly halted and returned to its place. The stunned spectators realized their rain-soaked clothes were totally dry! It was the Miracle of the Sun.

Pilgrimages to Fatima began in 1917, and on October 13, 1930, the Church officially approved the apparitions of Mary at Fatima. Pope Pius XII consecrated the world to the Immaculate Heart of Mary, as did Saint John Paul II on May 13, 1982.

Francisco Marto spent the rest of his short life in prayer and penance, dying of influenza in 1919. Jacinta died the next year, after suffering excruciatingly from a lung surgery, which she offered for sinners. Sister Lucia died in 2005. Francisco and Jacinta were beatified by Pope John Paul II on May 13th, 2000—the youngest non-martyrs ever to be beatified in the history of the Catholic Church! Pope John Paul II credited his miraculous escape from assassination to Our Lady of Fatima's intervention, and in 1989, Communism collapsed in Russia and Eastern Europe. Praise God!

The Fatima Message and First Saturday Devotion

At Fatima, Our Lady of the Rosary told the children that God had sent her with a message for every man, woman and child. Mary promised that Heaven would grant peace to the world if her requests for prayer, reparation, and consecration were heard and obeyed. Our Lady repeatedly emphasized the necessity of praying the Rosary daily, of wearing the Brown Scapular, and of performing acts of reparation and sacrifice.

She said, "I promise to help at the hour of death, with the graces needed for salvation, whoever on the First Saturday of five consecutive months shall:
- Confess and Receive Communion.
- Pray five decades of the Rosary
- Keep me company for fifteen minutes while meditating on the Mysteries of the Rosary, with the intention of making reparation to me."

Pope Saint John Paul II was shot by a would-be assassin on the feast of Our Lady of Fatima, May 13, 1982, and he credited his miraculous escape from death to her intervention.

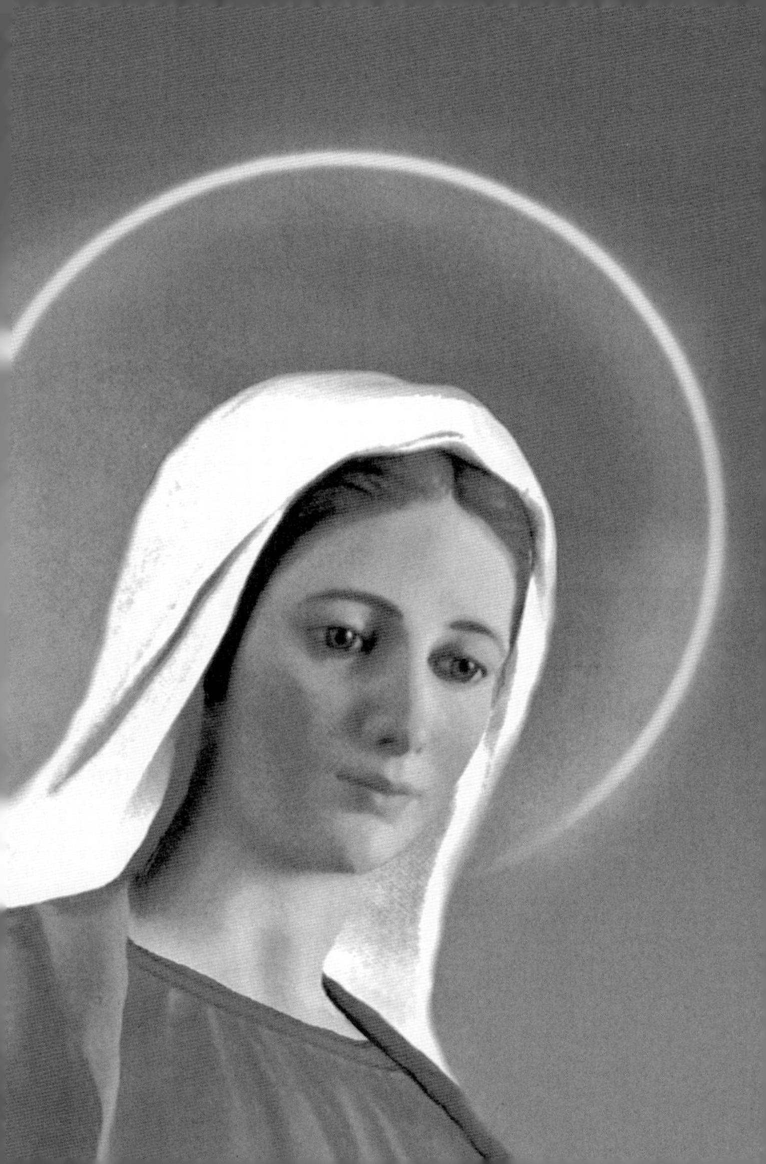

Our Lady of Medjugorje
Queen of Peace

(Editor's Note: As of the date of this publication, the Church is studying the alleged apparitions of our Lady at Medjugorje. When a final decision is made, we will most certainly abide by the Church's mandate.)

On the Balkan Peninsula lies the little country of Bosnia-Herzegovina, which harbors the tiny village of Medjugorje—"Between the Hills." It was here, on the feast of Saint John the Baptist in 1981, that six Croatian youths allegedly began receiving apparitions of the Blessed Virgin Mary—visitations that, for some of them, continue to this day.

On the night of June 24th, 1981, 16-year-old Mirjana Dragicevic and 15-year-old Ivanka Ivankovic noticed a mysterious bright light hovering over Mount Podbrdo in the hilly terrain of Medjugorje. In its rays they saw a beautiful young woman holding a baby. Frightened, the girls ran to the homes of their relatives. The next day, the two were joined by 9-year-old Jacov Colo, who lived with his ill mother, and Vicka Ivankovic, Marija Pavlovic, and Ivan Dragicevic, all of whom were 16 years old.

At the top of Mount Podbrdo, the children fell

to their knees in ecstasy as each one saw our Blessed Mother clearly. Our Lady was surrounded by an intense light and was crowned with twelve stars. She had dark hair covered by a luminous veil. Mary asked the children to return, and told them, "Go in the peace of God."

On the way down, Marija saw a radiant cross of light along a small path. Our Lady stood in front of the cross, weeping profusely. "Peace. Only peace! You must seek peace!" In that moment Marija gave her whole life to Our Blessed Mother.

Essentially, the visionaries tell us, Our Lady is calling each of us to a conversion of heart. She said that each person on earth seeks the gift of peace, which flows from a loving communion with God our Father.

During the past few decades, over 40 million pilgrims have journeyed to Medjugorje! Many have witnessed the miracle of the sun, similar to that miracle first seen at Fatima in October of 1917.

Others have experienced other supernatural phenomena. Our Lady told Vicka that these are signs that prayer changes hearts, circumstances, and endeavors. In a key message the Blessed Virgin said, "Do not be afraid, dear angels. I am the Mother of God. I am the Queen of Peace. I am the Mother of all People."

Our Lady has entrusted ten secrets to three of the visionaries: Mirjana, Ivanka, and Jacov. The other three visionaries have received nine secrets and continue to see Our Lady daily as they await the final one. According to Mirjana, they include chastisements for the wickedness of our world. The secrets will all come to pass in Mirjana's lifetime. Thus Mary calls us to prayer and penance, to deep inner conversion.

Our Blessed Mother Mary told the children that God has sent her to help humanity seek the immediate conversion of our hearts through fervent prayer. During what she calls this "Time of Grace," Mary in her messages is essentially giving us five directives:

- **Daily Prayer of the Rosary**
- **Monthly Confession**
- **Daily Reading of the Scripture**
- **Holy Mass**
- **Fasting**

With these "stones" we can defeat the enemy of our souls and allow God to bring forth in us His peace, the greatest good.

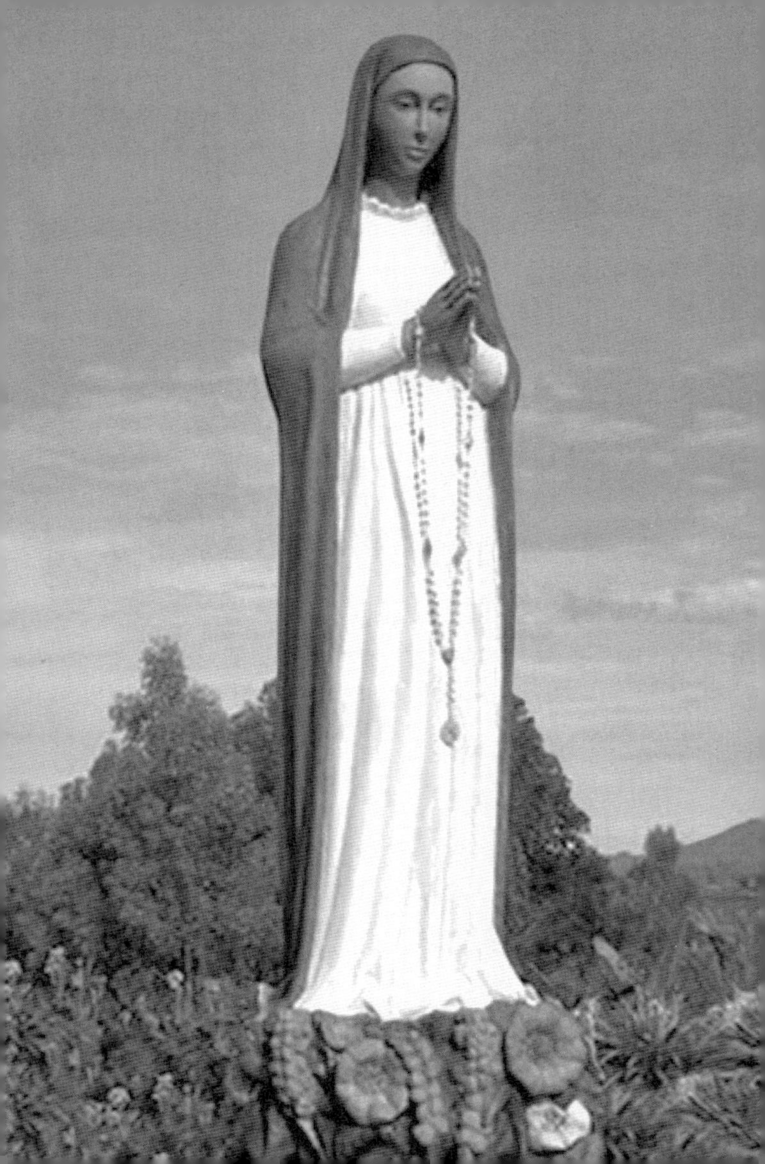

Our Lady of Kibeho
Our Lady of Sorrows

In the mountainous terrain of Rwanda, Africa lies the small, rather impoverished town of Kibeho. The Congregation of Benebikira Sisters (Daughters of the Virgin Mary) staff a Catholic school for girls in the town. On November 28, 1981, as 17-year-old Alphonsine Mumureke was serving tables during lunch, she heard a voice calling: "My daughter!" Going out to the corridor, Alphonsine saw a beautiful Lady. Alphonsine knelt instinctively and asked, "Who are you?" The Lady responded in Swahili, "I am Mother of the Word. I have heard your prayers. I would like you and your companions to have more faith. Some do not believe enough."

Our Lady appeared to Alphonsine in the days and weeks following. A few months later, Mary appeared to 17-year old Nathalie Mukamazimpaka. In March of 1982, 21-year-old Marie Claire Mukangango began seeing Our Lady as well. Others followed soon thereafter. Alphonsine, Nathalie, and Marie Claire alone received official approval of the Church. The visions to Alphonsine continued for exactly eight years, ending November 28th, 1989. Nathalie received visions until December, 1983, while Marie Claire's visions ended on September 15th, 1982. That same year, Bishop Gahamanyi appointed a medical and a theological commission to investigate the reports, and in 1988, approved the apparitions.

Alphonsine, who has since become a contemplative nun, laughed and cried during her visions. Often, when an apparition ended, she would faint from exhaustion. She described our Lady as wearing "a seamless white dress and also a white veil on her head. Her hands were clasped together on her breast, and her fingers pointed to the sky. ... I could not determine the color of her skin, but she was of incomparable beauty."

Our Lady explained to Marie Claire Mukangango, "When I show myself to someone and talk to them, I want to turn to the whole world. If I am now turning to the parish of Kibeho it does not mean I am only concerned for Kibeho or for the Diocese of Butare, or for Rwanda, or for the whole of Africa. I am concerned with and am turning to the whole world."

Mary asked Alphonsine and the other visionaries to prepare the world for the return of Jesus, and to convert as soon as possible. Alphonsine said that Mary told us to "be ready for our deaths and the end of the world."

Our Lady called the children, and the world, to pray the Rosary. She also requested that people would offer penance and fasting along with their prayers.

On August 19th, 1982, a crowd of 20,000 people from all over Africa came to the school for an expected apparition. Microphones had been set up to record any messages from the Virgin Mary. Alphonsine went into ecstasy and began to sing a song of welcome to Our Lady. However, the Blessed Mother cut her off, saying, "I am too sad to hear my children sing." After some moments of silence, Mary began to weep.

Upon seeing Our Lady so distraught, Alphonsine also began to sob uncontrollably before the huge crowd. Three times she repeated into the microphone, "You opened the door and they refused to come in." Suddenly Alphonsine screamed and cried, "I see a river of blood!"

Later Alphonsine and the other visionaries testified to an ecclesiastical commission that on that August day, Our Blessed Mother had revealed to them numerous disturbing images of destruction and torture. She showed them bodies chopped by machetes, piling up on the ground. These images from the future increased until Alphonsine saw a huge pile of headless corpses rotting in a valley. Alphonsine fell to her knees often during the vision, crying, "On the day you will come to call your children, have mercy on us!"

The visionaries all belonged to the Tutsi tribe,

a minority tribe in Rwanda, which was ruled by the larger Hutu tribe. The Tutsi had been in power for centuries, until 1962. On April 6th, 1994, Hutu extremists assassinated Rwanda President Juvénal Habyarimana, touching off a 100-day genocide in which 800,000 Rwandans, mainly minority Tutsis, were murdered.

Visionary Marie Clare was among the slain Tutsis. One year later, in reprisal, 2,000 Hutus who had taken refuge at a camp in Kibeho were killed at the very spot of Mary's apparitions. The blood flowed like a river.

Our Lady warned the visionaries of coming global disasters, if the world did not turn to her and her Son. Even so, Alphonsine shared, "She loves us—that's what I feel the most when she's with me. ... Imagine how much your Mom loves you, and then multiply that love a million times."

Our Blessed Mother beseeched the visionaries, and the world, to pray the Rosary every day, especially the Seven Sorrows Rosary, which includes the mysteries of Simeon's Prophecy, the Flight into Egypt, the Loss of Jesus in the Temple, the meeting of Jesus and Mary on the Way to Calvary, the Crucifixion, the taking down of Jesus from the Cross, and the Burial of Jesus.

In 1990, Saint John Paul II visited Rwanda. He called the faithful to turn to Our Blessed Mother as a simple and sure guide, and to pray against political and ethnic divisions. Two years later, work began on a shrine to Our Lady of Sorrows in Kibeho. On June 29, 2001, Bishop Augustine Misago declared the apparitions at Kibeho to be authentic. Today, thousands of pilgrims visit the shrine annually, to remember and pray to Our Mother—Our Lady—of Sorrows.

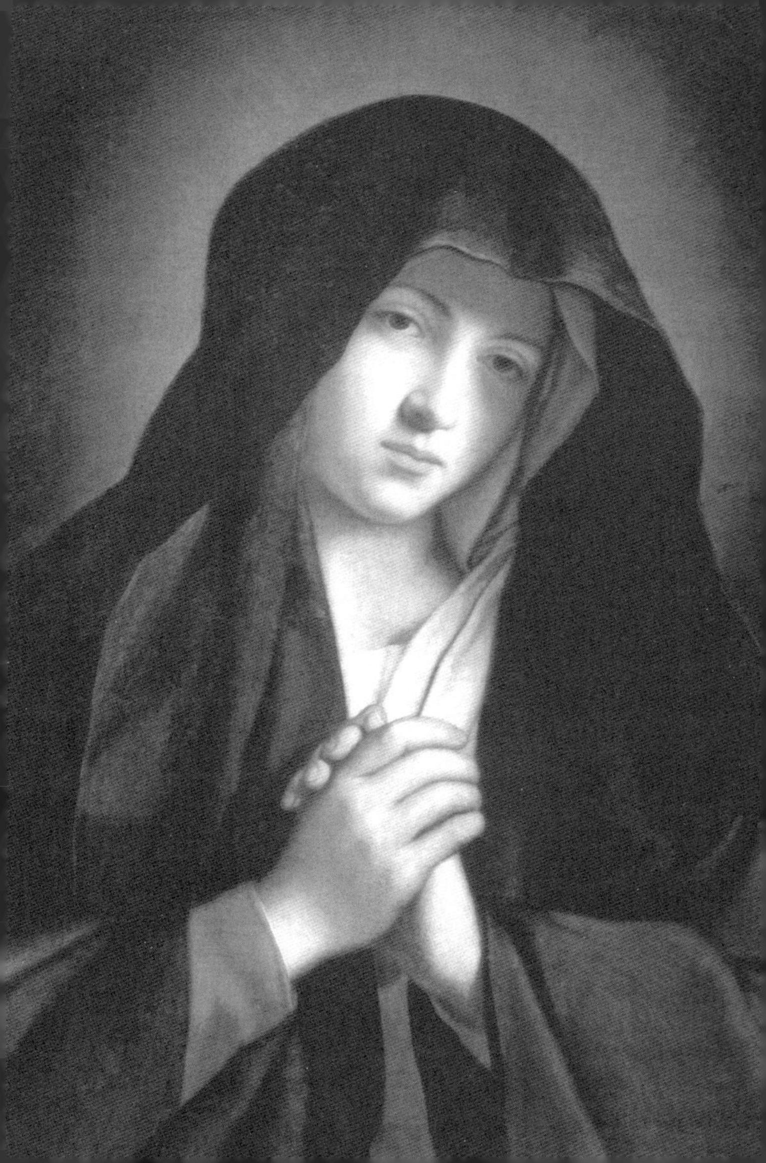

The Sorrows of Mary

Saint Gianna Molla said, "One cannot love without suffering or suffer without loving." Next to Jesus, Mary loves us with the deepest fervor and most compassionate earnestness, as she loves her Son. And in both cases, she has suffered and suffers still.

To suffer is to endure—pain, loss, or distress. Sorrow is the mental and emotional anguish that suffering causes. When Mary accepted God's gracious invitation to become the mother of His Son, though she did not fully understand or realize what this would mean, she humbly and willingly said, "Behold, I am the handmaid of the Lord. May it be done to me according to your word" (Luke 1:38). Mary responded in faith, not unlike Abraham, our "father in faith," who believed God when he too was promised a son, though it appeared impossible by natural means.

As Mary lived out her "Fiat" to God, she encountered arduous sufferings and sorrows, as well as profound joys. For instance, when she and Joseph went up to the Temple for the joyful presentation of Jesus to the Lord, she also heard the prophetic, yet enigmatic, words of Simeon: "Behold, this child is destined for the fall and rise of many in Israel, and to be a sign that will be contradicted (and you yourself a sword will pierce) so that the thoughts of many hearts may be revealed" (Luke 2:34-35).

Mary listened first, both to the angel Gabriel at the Annunciation, and to Simeon at the Presentation. Then she reflected, considering within herself what she both saw and heard. Mary prayed, asking God for wisdom to discern His will. Then she acted. She moved forward to embrace God's Will, whatever He had planned for her, confident that He would work all things out according to His Will.

Mary is thus an example for us, her children. She teaches us how to walk through the inevitable sufferings and sorrows that we have to face as we too travel with her toward the kingdom. She teaches us to listen, with an open heart, and to ponder what *we* see and hear. She teaches us to respond in faith, trusting that God is truly our good, good, Father, even when we feel separate or even abandoned by Him.

Mary teaches us to remain in the Will of God, rather than seek to escape the cross in our life. Even more, Mary teaches us to trust that God will work through the cross for our ultimate good and the good of others. But she doesn't stop there. As a true mother, Mary gives us her heart, to strengthen us so that we might continue *through* the cross to the Resurrection.

The Promises of Mary's Seven Sorrows

According to Saint Bridget of Sweden, our Blessed Mother Mary promised to grant seven graces to those who honor her and draw near to her and her Son every day by meditating on her sorrows.

1. "I will grant peace to their families."
2. "They will be enlightened about the divine Mysteries."
3. "I will console them in their pains and will accompany them in their work."
4. "I will give them as much as they ask for as long as it does not oppose the adorable will of my divine Son or the sanctification of their souls."
5. "I will defend them in their spiritual battles with the infernal enemy and I will protect them at every instant of their lives."
6. "I will visibly help them at the moment of their death—they will see the face of their mother."
7. "I have obtained this grace from my divine Son, that those who propagate this devotion to my tears and dolors will be taken directly from this earthly life to eternal happiness, since all their sins will be forgiven and my Son will be their eternal consolation and joy."

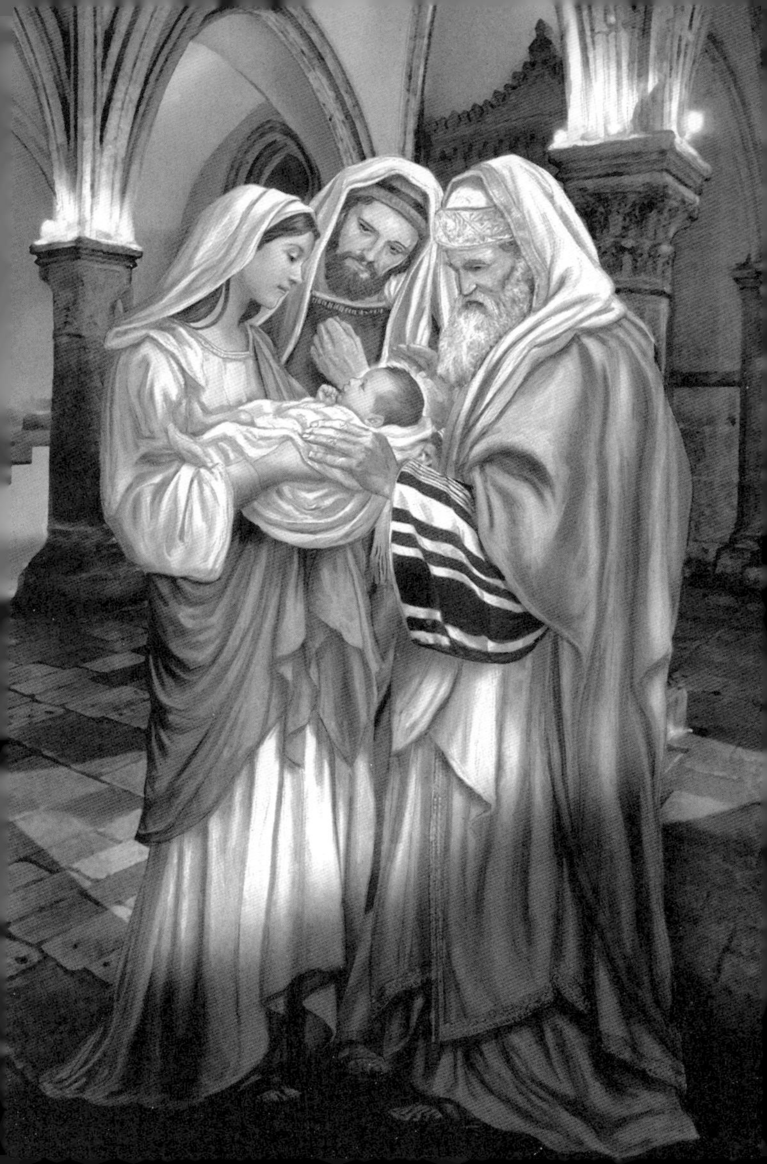

FIRST SORROW
The Presentation of the Child Jesus

Joseph and Mary brought their newborn son, Jesus, to the temple in Jerusalem as the Law required. There they met a devout old man named Simeon who, led by the Holy Spirit, prophesied to Mary what her child would become.

Joy and astonishment thrilled the hearts of Mary and Joseph as they listened to Simeon's wondrous announcement and received his blessing. However, no joy is perfect on this earth. Simeon turned to Mary and said, "Behold, this child is destined for the fall and rise of many in Israel, and to be a sign that will be contradicted (and you yourself a sword will pierce) so that the thoughts of many hearts may be revealed" (Luke 2:34-35).

Although Mary was deeply touched by the favor given her by God to bear His Son, the Savior of the world, her heart remained heavy and troubled, for she knew what was written about the Suffering Servant of God, the Messiah. Mary would be grieved by the widespread rejection her Son would face. Yet she resolutely moved forward, confident that the God who had called her would be her support to the end.

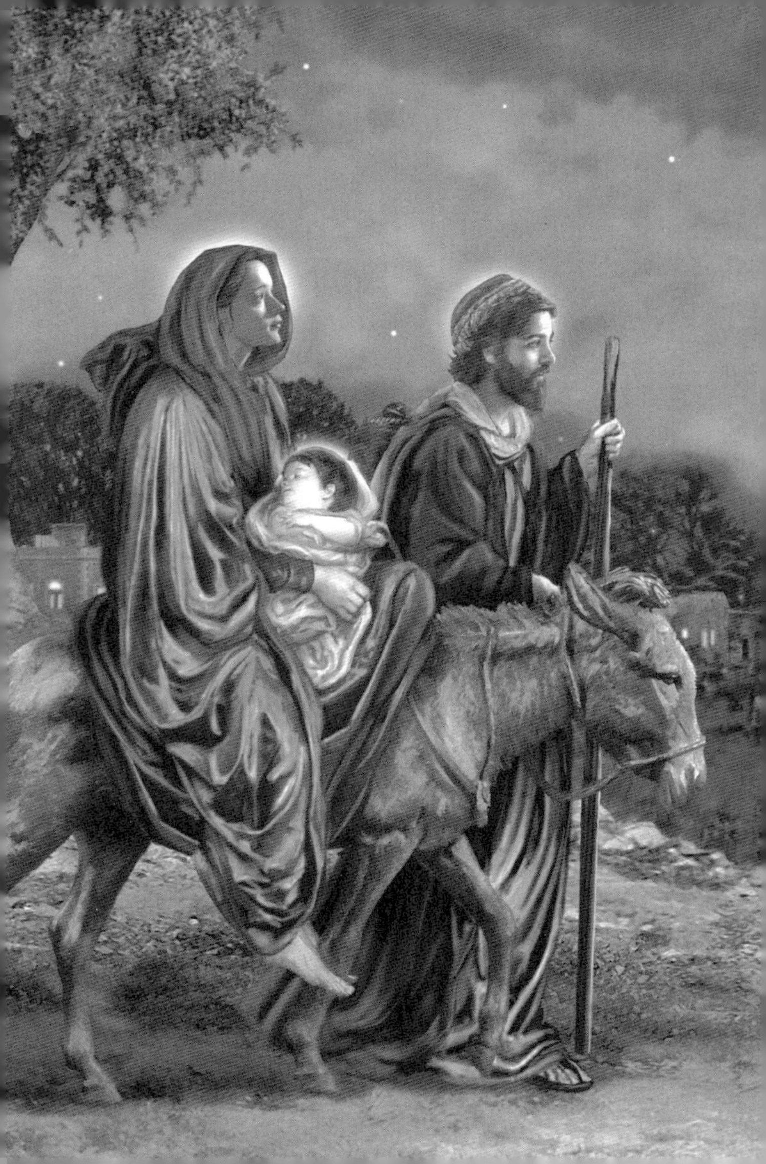

SECOND SORROW
The Flight into Egypt

Some time later, the angel of the Lord warned Joseph in a dream that Herod's men were in search of the Holy Child to kill Him. Mary and Joseph needed to leave at once with the infant Jesus and take Him to Egypt for refuge.

Because the Blessed Virgin was the Mother of Jesus, she loved Him more than anyone else. Her heart remained constantly anguished during this long and arduous flight through the wild, bandit-infested desert into a heathen country. The sword was piercing her heart, but the babe was pressing against the wounds. He and His mother had made their sacrifice; they had laid themselves on the altar as victims, and were already being consumed.

Mary's thoughts centered only on her Son's safety and comfort. Though indeed the Holy Family very likely endured sufferings, both on the journey as well as in that land of exile, they obeyed promptly, generously, and without complaint. They obeyed because Jesus was with them, and they knew that with Him, they could overcome all difficulties.

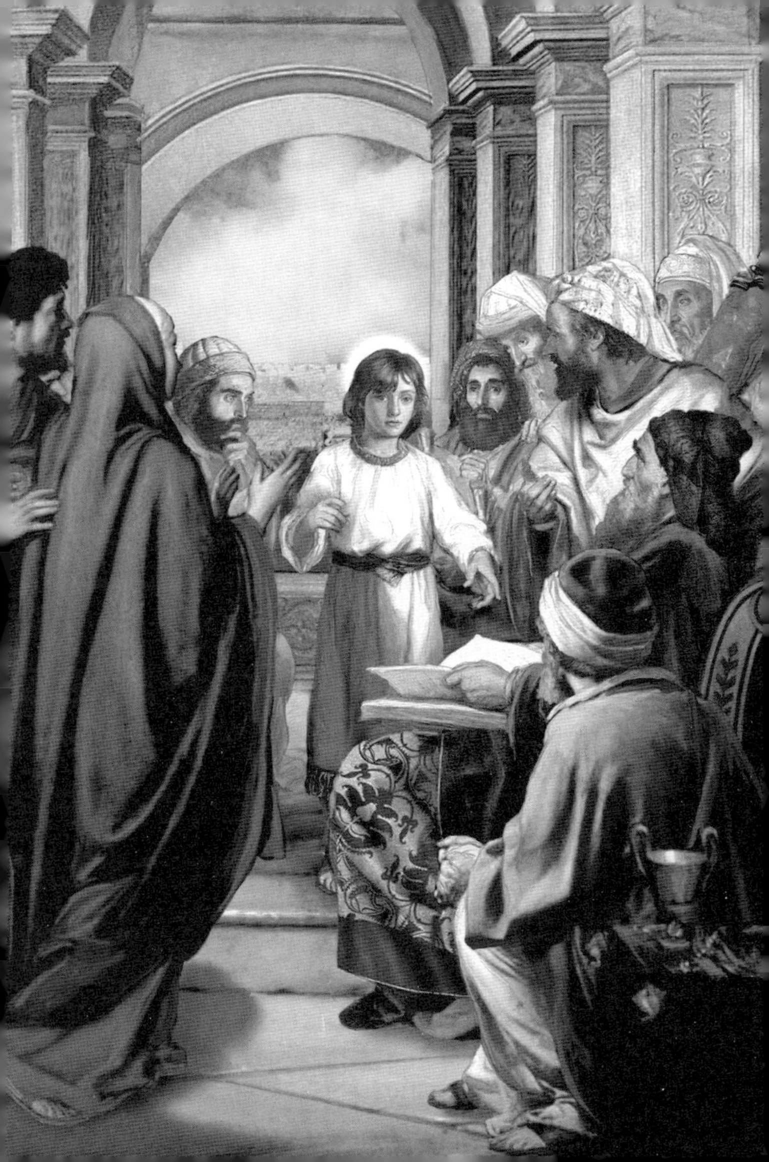

THIRD SORROW
The Three Days' Loss of the Divine Child

Jesus was God's only begotten Son, and also the Virgin Mary's son. The Blessed Virgin loved Jesus more than herself because He was her God. Compared to other children, Jesus was a unique child because He was already living as God.

When Mary and Joseph discovered that Jesus was missing on their journey home from Jerusalem, how dreadful was Mary's grief. Fear gripped her as alarming thoughts ran through her mind about what might have happened to her beloved Son. As Mary searched anxiously and frantically for Jesus, deep pain welled up inside her. She also ached at the sight of her beloved spouse, Joseph, who was so deeply pained as he and Mary tirelessly sought their son.

Mary was especially grieved that her Son had decided to stay behind without her consent. In this sense, Mary felt a pain similar to that of Jesus when He was abandoned by His apostles during His Passion. Finally, on the third day, Joseph and Mary found Jesus in the temple with the doctors of the Law.

Mary teaches us that we too, must seek the Lord while He may be found, with all our hearts. We also must learn to wait upon the Lord with trust. He will raise us up, on eagles' wings.

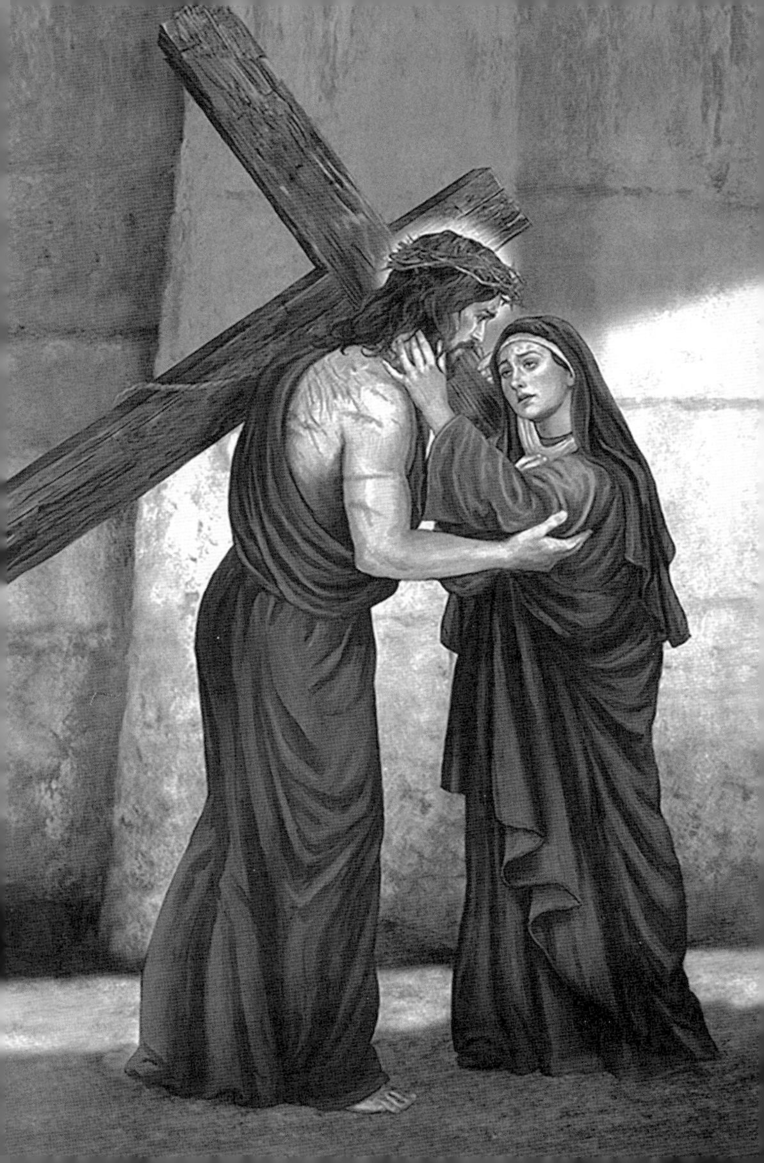

FOURTH SORROW
Mary Meets Jesus Carrying the Cross

The Blessed Virgin met Jesus staggering under the heavy weight of the cross on which He was to be crucified. In this meeting, Mary experienced one of the most unbearable situations that a mother could ever know. She was filled with anguish and heartbreak when she saw her Son so weakened by the numerous hard blows given by the soldiers' clubs, with His blood streaming down into His eyes from His thorn-crowned head and trickling from the deep wounds on His scourged back.

Mary yearned to clasp her arms around her son, to shield Him from the deceit of the enemy; but she knew that "He must be about His Father's business." He had come to fulfill His mission as Redeemer, and in order to participate in His work, Mary had to sacrifice a mother's most tender and sacred feelings.

When Jesus' eyes met Mary's, their looks became as so many arrows that wounded their hearts, for they loved each other tenderly and totally.

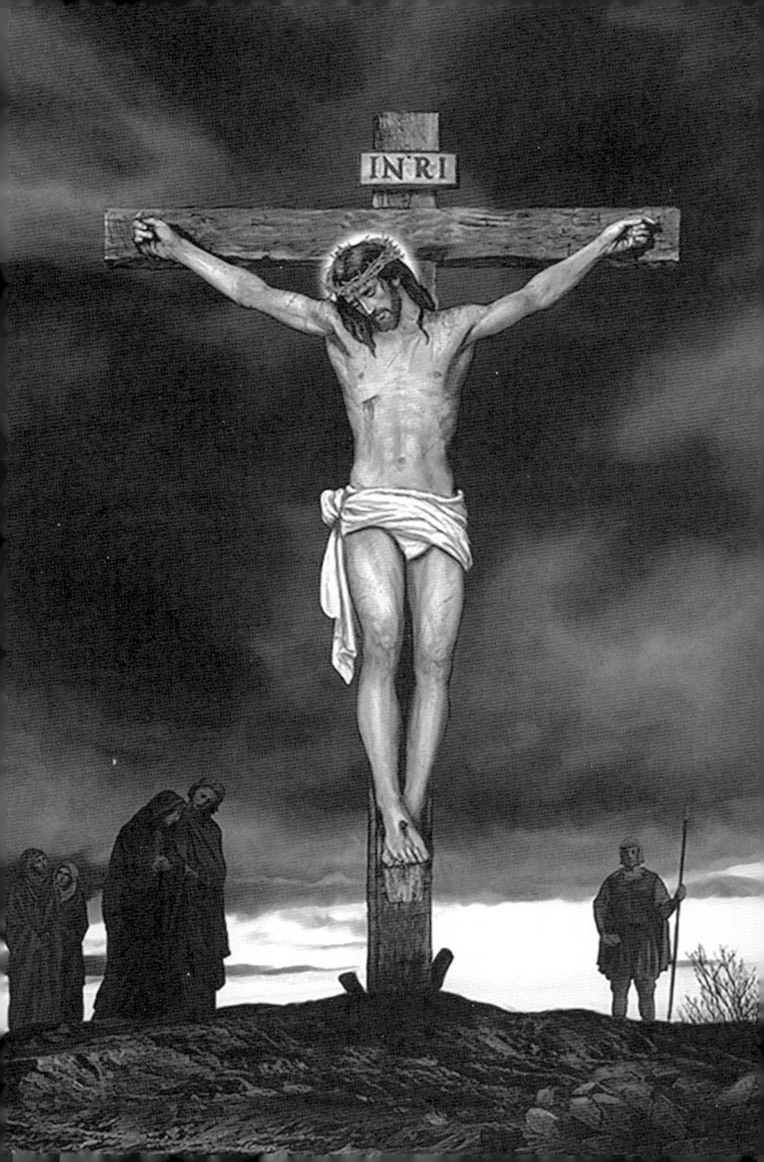
IN RI

FIFTH SORROW
The Crucifixion of Mary's Divine Son

The Blessed Virgin Mary continued to climb the mount to Calvary, following behind Jesus in pain and sorrow, suffering in silence. Mary witnessed how the soldiers roughly tore the garments off His body so that the skin came with them.

When they laid Jesus naked on the cross, the Blessed Virgin felt sick at heart. As her Son's torturers drove the nails through Jesus' hands and feet, Mary felt the blows in her heart. She felt her life fading away, for her heart and soul were also crucified together with her Son. She couldn't do anything for Him. Her dreadful helplessness only added to the inexpressible grief of her maternal heart.

Mary felt all of Jesus' sufferings and offered them for the honor of God and the salvation of men. During her vigil at the cross, the words Jesus uttered would ring down the ages as a word of love for Mary, and as a legacy of love for man: "Woman, behold your son." Turning to John, the beloved disciple, Jesus then said, "Behold your Mother."

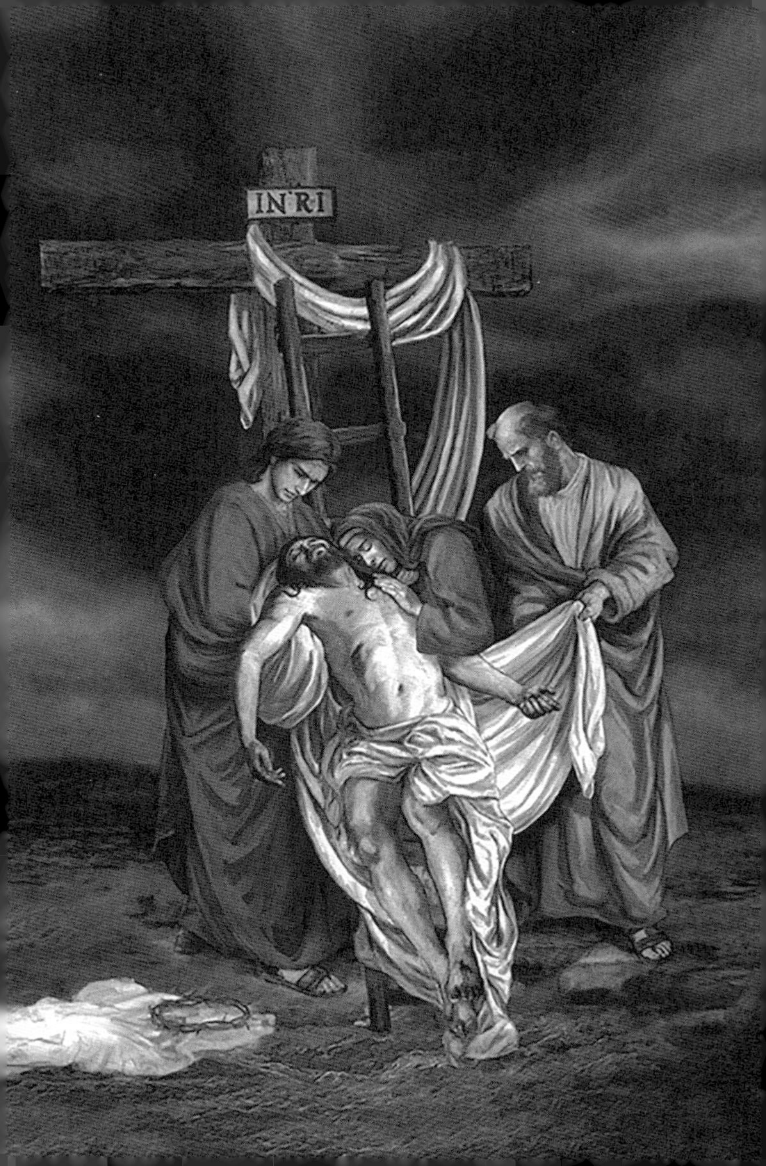
INRI

SIXTH SORROW
The Body of Jesus is Taken Down from the Cross

The sacrifice on the Cross was consummated. The last drop of blood trickled from our Redeemer's heart. Joseph of Arimathea and Nicodemus slowly and reverently lowered the sacred body of Jesus from the Cross and placed it on the Blessed Virgin's lap. Mary held her Son in her arms and let His head recline upon her bosom.

She silently contemplated the bloody and broken body of Jesus and washed it with deep respect and love because she was His Mother. She knew better than anyone else that He was God Incarnate who had come to this world to become the Savior of all. Mary saw the horrifying wounds from the flogging Jesus had received, His torn flesh, gaping wounds, and the wound on His head that had penetrated His brain.

As the Queen of Martyrs, Mary freely offered her Son, who had come to save the human race, back to His Father. As Saint Bernard would later write, "The measure of love for God is to love Him without measure."

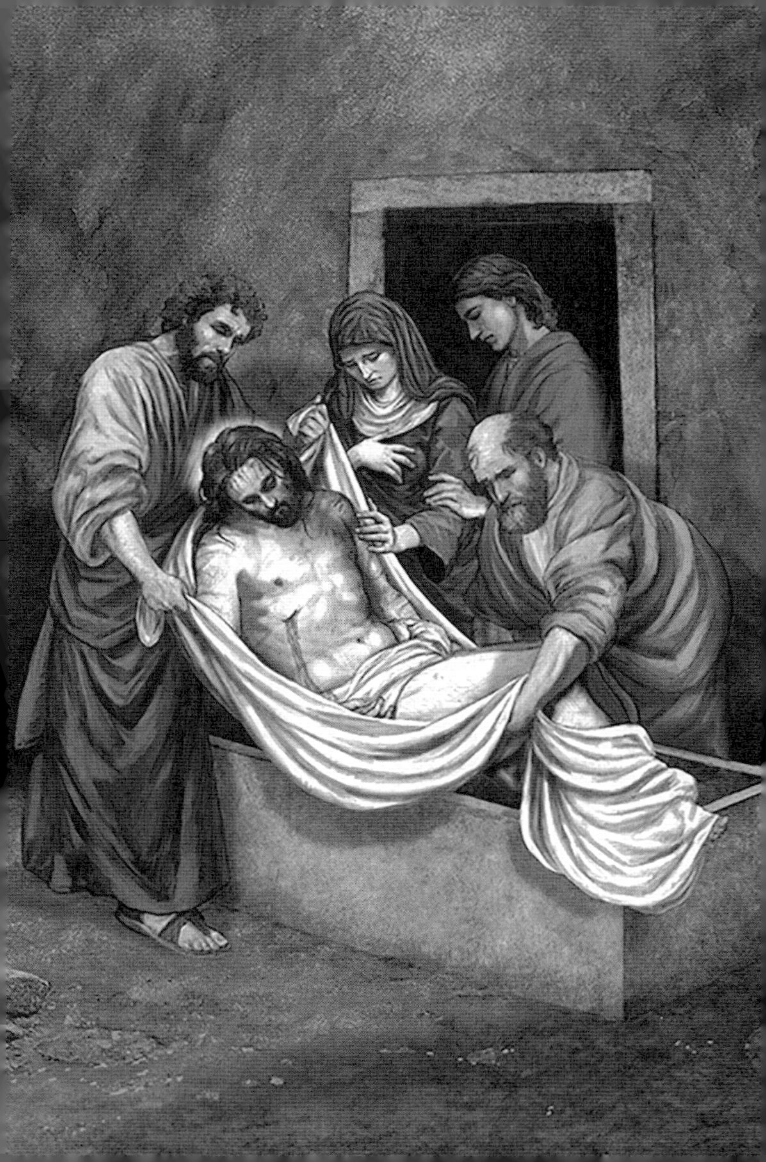

SEVENTH SORROW
The Body of Jesus is Laid in the Tomb

With a gentle care and deep sorrow, the friends of Jesus prepared His divine body for burial. They did everything in their power to show their reverence for our Savior. They bought the finest linen, while Nicodemus brought "a mixture of myrrh and aloes, about a hundred pounds' weight."

The life of the Blessed Virgin Mary was intimately linked to that of Jesus. Her only consolation in His death was that all His unspeakable sufferings had come to an end.

Our sorrowful Mother, with the help of Saint John, Nicodemus, Joseph of Arimathea, and the holy women, devoutly placed Jesus' body in the sepulcher. Mary then went home with John, in great pain, her heart pierced and torn with the sharpest grief, dying at heart with her Son Jesus, but yet burning with the ardent hope that He would rise again.

This, we name her Seventh Sorrow—the indescribable desolation which she took upon herself, for love of us; the stupendous yearning for her Son who went before her.

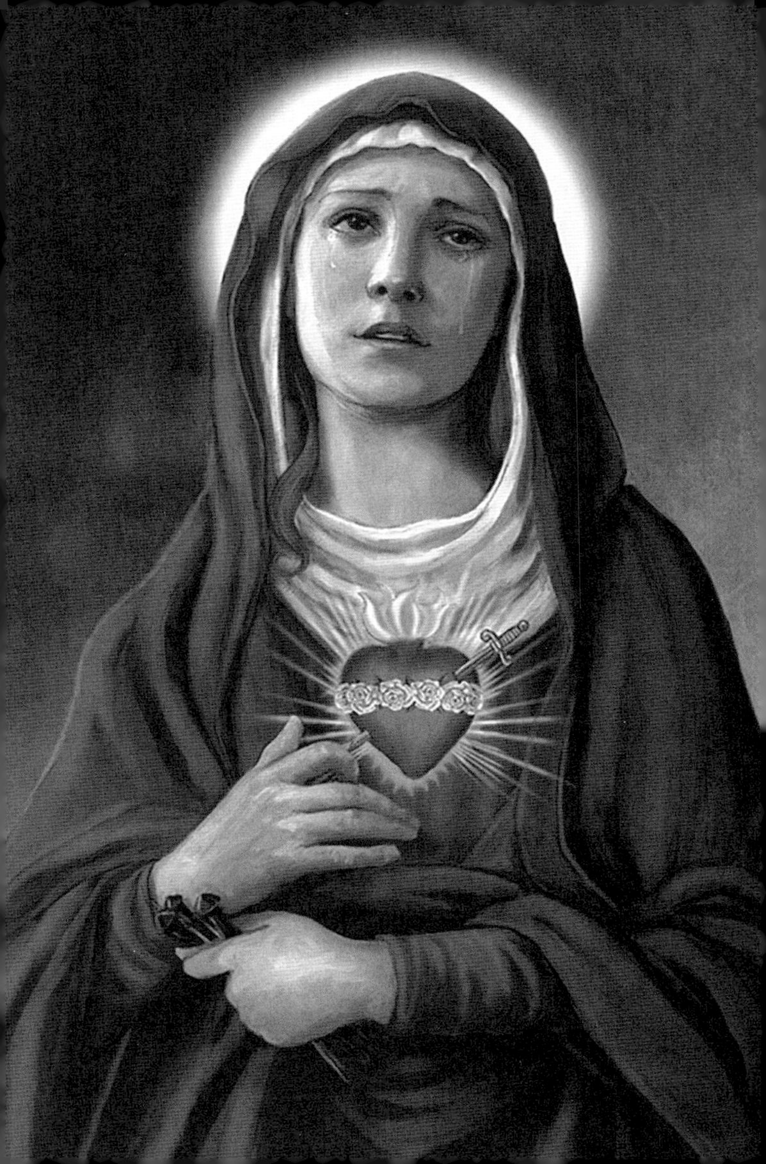

An Act of Consecration to Our Sorrowful Mother

Holy Mary, Mother of God and Queen of Martyrs, today I choose you as my model, Protectress, and advocate. In your Immaculate Heart, pierced with so many swords of sorrow, I place my soul forever. Receive me as your special servant, as a partaker in your sufferings. Give me strength always to remain close to that Cross on which your only Son died for me. All that I am and have, I consecrate to your service. Accept every good work that I may perform and offer it to your Son for me. Dear Mother, help me to be worthy of the title: "Servant of Mary."

Stand by me in all my actions that they may be directed to the glory of God. As you were close to Christ, your Son, on the Cross, be near to me, your child, in my last agony. Obtain for me, that I may invoke your and His sweet name, saying with my lips and my heart: "Jesus, Mary, and Joseph, assist me in my last agony. Jesus, Mary, and Joseph, may I die in peace in your holy company." Amen.

The Novena in Honor of the Seven Sorrows of Mary

V. O God, come to my assistance.
R. O Lord, make haste to help me.
V. Glory be to the Father, and to the Son, and to the Holy Spirit.
R. As it was in the beginning, is now, and ever shall be, world without end. Amen.

For the First Sorrow
The Prophecy of Simeon

I grieve for you, O Mary most sorrowful, in the affliction of your tender heart at the prophecy of the holy and aged Simeon. Dear Mother, by your heart so afflicted, obtain for me the virtue of humility and the gift of the holy fear of God.
Pray one Hail Mary.

For the Second Sorrow
The Flight into Egypt

I grieve for you, O Mary most sorrowful, in the anguish of your most affectionate heart during the flight into Egypt and your sojourn there. Dear Mother,

by your heart so troubled, obtain for me the virtue of generosity, especially toward the poor, and the gift of piety.
Pray one Hail Mary.

For the Third Sorrow
The Loss of the Child Jesus in the Temple

I grieve for you, O Mary most sorrowful, in those anxieties which tried your troubled heart at the loss of your dear Jesus. Dear Mother, by your heart so full of anguish, obtain for me the virtue of chastity and the gift of knowledge.
Pray one Hail Mary.

For the Fourth Sorrow
Mary Meets Jesus on the Way to Calvary

I grieve for you, O Mary most sorrowful, in the consternation of your heart at meeting Jesus as He carried His cross. Dear Mother, by your heart so troubled, obtain for me the virtue of patience and the gift of fortitude.
Pray one Hail Mary.

For the Fifth Sorrow
Mary Stands at the Foot of the Cross

I grieve for you O Mary, most sorrowful, in the Martyrdom which your generous heart endured in standing near Jesus in His agony. Dear Mother, by your afflicted heart, obtain for me the virtue of temperance and the gift of counsel.
Pray one Hail Mary.

For the Sixth Sorrow
Mary Receives the Dead Body of Jesus in Her Arms

I grieve for you, O Mary most sorrowful, in the wounding of your compassionate heart, when the side of Jesus was struck by the lance and His Heart was pierced before His body was removed from the Cross. Dear Mother, by your heart thus transfixed, obtain for me the virtue of fraternal charity and the gift of understanding.
Pray one Hail Mary.

For the Seventh Sorrow
Jesus is Placed in the Tomb

I grieve for you, O Mary most sorrowful, for the pangs that wrenched your most loving heart at the burial of Jesus. Dear Mother, by your heart sunk in the sorrow of desolation, obtain for me the virtue of diligence and the gift of wisdom.
Pray one Hail Mary.

V. Pray for us, O Virgin most sorrowful.
R. That we may be made worthy of the promises of Christ.

Let us Pray: Intercede for us, we beg You, O Lord Jesus Christ, now and at the hour of our death, before the throne of Your mercy, by the Blessed Virgin Mary, Your Mother, whose most holy soul was pierced by a sword of sorrow in the hour of Your bitter Passion. We ask this through You, Jesus Christ, Savior of the world, Who lives and reigns with the Father and the Holy Spirit, world without end. Amen.

Litany of Our Lady of Sorrows
(For Private Devotion)

V. Lord, have mercy on us.
R. Christ, have mercy on us.
V. Lord, have mercy on us. Christ, hear us.
R. Christ, graciously hear us.
V. God, the Father of heaven,
R. Have mercy on us.
V. God the Son, Redeemer of the world,
R. Have mercy on us.
V. God the Holy Spirit,
R. Have mercy on us.
Mother of Sorrows, **R. Pray for us.***
Mother whose soul was pierced by the sword,*
Mother who fled with Jesus into Egypt,*
Mother who sought Him sorrowing for three days,*
Mother who saw Him scourged and crowned with thorns,*
Mother who stood by Him while He hung upon the Cross,*
Mother who received Him into your arms when He was dead,*
Mother who saw Him buried in the tomb,*
O Mary, Queen of Martyrs, **R. Save us by your prayers.***

O Mary, comfort of the sorrowful, **R. Save us by your prayers.**
O Mary, help of the weak,*
O Mary, strength of the fearful,*
O Mary, light of the despondent,*
O Mary, nursing mother of the sick,*
O Mary, refuge of sinners,*
Through the bitter Passion of your Son,*
Through the piercing anguish of your heart,*
Through your heavy weight of woe,*
Through your sadness and desolation,*
Through your maternal pity,*
Through your perfect resignation,*
Through your meritorious prayers,*
From immoderate sadness,*
From a cowardly spirit,*
From an impatient temper,*
From fretfulness and discontent,*
From sullenness and gloom,*
From despair and unbelief,*
From final impenitence,*

Preserve us from sudden death, **R. We beseech you, hear us.***
Teach us how to die,*
Help us in our last agony,*

Guard us from the enemy, **R. We beseech you, hear us.**
Bring us to a happy end,*
Gain for us the gift of perseverance,*
Aid us before the Judgment Seat,*
Mother of God,*
Mother, most sorrowful,*
Mother, most desolate,*

V. Lamb of God, You take away the sins of the world,
R. Spare us, O Lord.
V. Lamb of God, You take away the sins of the world,
R. Graciously hear us, O Lord.
V. Lamb of God, You take away the sins of the world,
R. Have mercy on us.
V. Christ, hear us.
R. Christ, graciously hear us.
V. Lord, have mercy.
R. Christ, have mercy.
V. Lord, have mercy.
V. Help us, O Blessed Virgin Mary,
R. In every time, and in every place.

Let Us Pray: O Lord Jesus Christ, God and Man, grant, we beseech You, that Your dear Mother Mary, whose soul the sword pierced in the hour of Your

Passion, may intercede for us, now, and in the hour of our death, through Your own merits, O Savior of the world, who with the Father and the Holy Spirit lives and reigns, God, world without end. Amen.

Prayer to Mary, Our Lady of Sorrows
by St. Bonaventure

O most holy virgin, mother of our Lord Jesus Christ: by the overwhelming grief you experienced when you witnessed the martyrdom, the crucifixion, and the death of your divine Son, look upon me with eyes of compassion and awaken in my heart a tender commiseration for those sufferings, as well as a sincere detestation of my sins, in order that, being disengaged from all undue affections for the passing joys of this earth, I may long for the eternal Jerusalem, and that henceforth all my thoughts and all my actions may be directed toward this one most desirable object. Honor, glory, and love to our divine Lord Jesus, and to the holy and immaculate mother of God.
Amen.

The Angelus

The Angelus is a venerable devotion to Our Lady—from the Latin: *Angelus Domini nuntiavit Mariae*. The Angelus began as a morning greeting to Mary. Later, the practice of praying a Hail Mary at evening spread throughout Christendom. In 1456, Pope Callistus III ordered that bells be rung at noon and Hail Marys prayed for the success of the Crusades.

V. The Angel of the Lord declared unto Mary.

R. And she conceived by the Holy Spirit. *(Hail Mary)*

V. Behold the handmaid of the Lord.

R. Be it done unto me according to thy word. *(Hail Mary)*

V. And the Word was made Flesh.

R. And dwelt among us. *(Hail Mary)*

V. Pray for us, O Holy Mother of God.

R. That we may be made worthy of the promises of Christ.

Let us pray: Pour forth, we beseech Thee, O Lord, Thy grace into our hearts; that we to whom the Incarnation of Christ, Thy Son, was made known by the message of an Angel, may by His Passion and Cross, be brought to the glory of His Resurrection. Through the same Christ our Lord. Amen.

Regina Coeli
(Queen of Heaven)

V. O Queen of Heaven, rejoice, Alleluia.
R. For He whom you were made worthy to bear, Alleluia.
V. Has risen as He said, Alleluia.
R. Pray for us to God, Alleluia.
V. Rejoice and be glad, O Virgin Mary! Alleluia.
R. For the Lord is truly risen, Alleluia.

Let us pray: O God, who by the Resurrection of your Son, our Lord Jesus Christ, granted joy to the whole world: grant, we beg you, that through the intercession of the Virgin Mary, His Mother, we may lay hold of the joys of eternal life. Through the same Christ our Lord. Amen.

In 1724, Pope Benedict approved the Angelus and Regina Coeli (prayed during Easter).

Novenas

Before His ascension into heaven, Jesus directed His apostles to wait and pray for the coming of the Holy Spirit. With Mary, they prayed in Jerusalem for nine days. The next morning, Pentecost, they were all filled with the Holy Spirit and the Church was born. In later years, the practice of praying nine days for a special intention developed. This devotion was called a novena, from the Latin word for nine: *novem*.

A novena, then, refers to devotions which take place over nine consecutive days or, in some cases, one day a week over nine consecutive weeks. Through the many novenas prayed down the long ages of the Church, believers have sought for and found help, relief, and peace from God.

Jesus told us, "Therefore I tell you, all that you ask for in prayer, believe that you will receive and it shall be yours." The Church calls her children to pray novenas as they are to pray all prayers, with faith in a gracious and loving Father who cares for them and is working out His Will in their lives.

Novena to Our Lady of the Miraculous Medal

Pray the following prayers daily for nine days:

Come Holy Spirit, fill the hearts of Your faithful and kindle in them the fire of Your love.
V. Send forth Your Spirit, and they shall be created.
R. And You shall renew the face of the earth.

Let us pray: O God, Who has instructed the hearts of the faithful by the light of the Holy Spirit, grant us in the same Spirit to be truly wise, and ever to rejoice in His consolation. Through Jesus Christ our Lord. Amen.

O Mary, conceived without sin,
Pray for us who have recourse to you.
(Three times)

O Lord Jesus Christ, who has glorified Your Mother, the Blessed Virgin Mary, immaculate from the first moment of her conception, grant that all who devoutly implore her protection on earth may eternally enjoy Your presence in heaven.

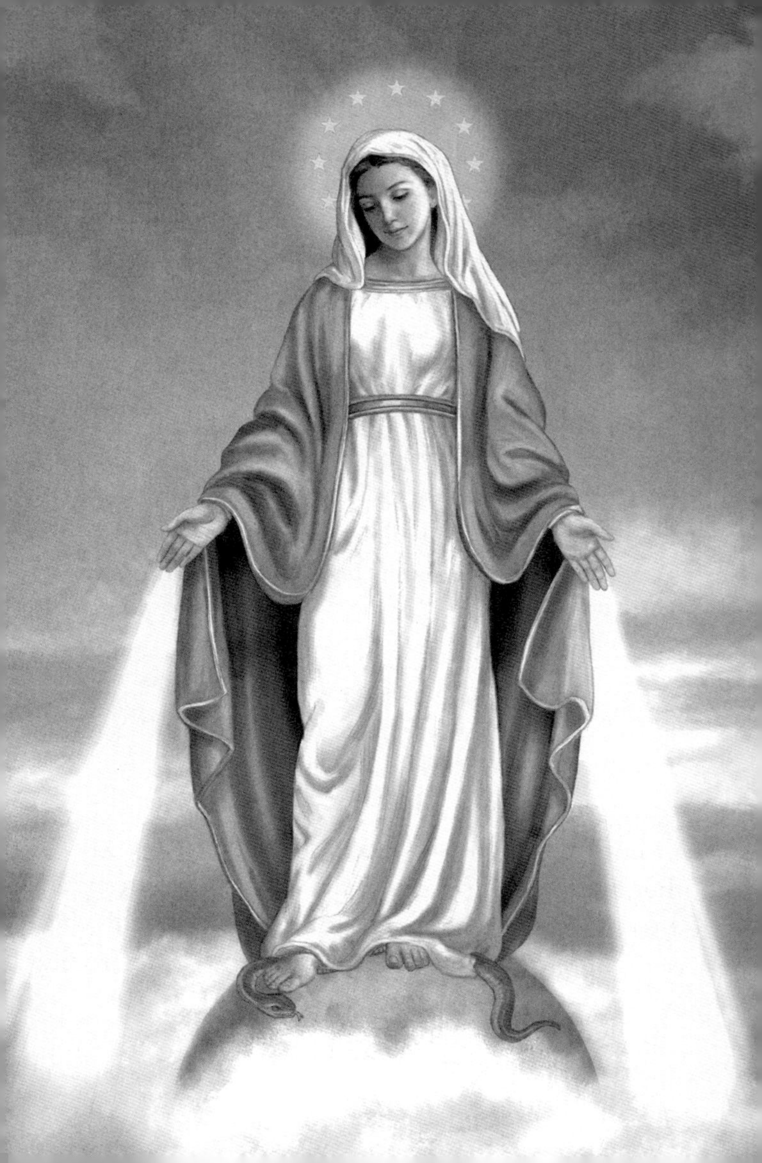

O Lord Jesus Christ, who for the accomplishment of Your greatest works have chosen the weak things of the world, that no flesh may glory in Your sight, and who for a better and more widely diffused belief in the Immaculate Conception of Your Mother, have wished that the Miraculous Medal be manifested to Saint Catherine Labouré, grant, we ask You, that filled with like humility, we may glorify this mystery by word and work. Amen.

The Memorare

Remember, O most gracious Virgin Mary, that never was it known, that anyone who fled to your protection, implored your assistance, or sought your intercession, was left unaided.

Inspired with this confidence, I fly unto you, O Virgin of Virgins, my Mother; to you I come; before you I kneel sinful and sorrowful. O Mother of the Word Incarnate, despise not my petitions, but in your mercy hear and answer them. Amen.

Novena Prayer

O Immaculate Virgin Mary, mother of our Lord Jesus and our mother, we have confidence in your powerful and never-failing intercession, manifested so often through the Miraculous Medal. We, your loving and trustful children, ask you to obtain for us the graces and favors we ask during this novena if they will be for the glory of God and the salvation of souls. *(Mention your request).*

You know, O Mary, how often our souls have been the sanctuaries of your Son who hates iniquity. Obtain for us then, a deep hatred of sin and that purity of heart which will attach us to God alone so that our every thought, word, and deed may tend to His greater glory.

Obtain for us also a spirit of prayer and self-denial that we may recover by penance what we have lost by sin and at length attain to that blessed abode where you are the Queen of angels and of men. Amen.

Consecration to Our Lady of the Miraculous Medal

O Virgin Mother of God, Mary Immaculate, we consecrate ourselves to you under your title of Our Lady of the Miraculous Medal. May this medal be for each one of us a sure sign of your motherly affection for us and a constant reminder of our filial duties towards you. While wearing it, may we be blessed by your loving protection and preserved in the grace of your Son. Most powerful Virgin, Mother of our Savior, keep us close to you every moment of our lives so that, like you, we may live and act according to the teaching and example of your Son.

Obtain for us, your children, the grace of a happy death so that in union with you we may enjoy the happiness of heaven forever. Amen.

O Mary, conceived without sin,
Pray for us who have recourse to you.

Closing Prayer

O Mary conceived without sin, pray for us:
O Mary conceived without sin, pray for us who have recourse to thee.

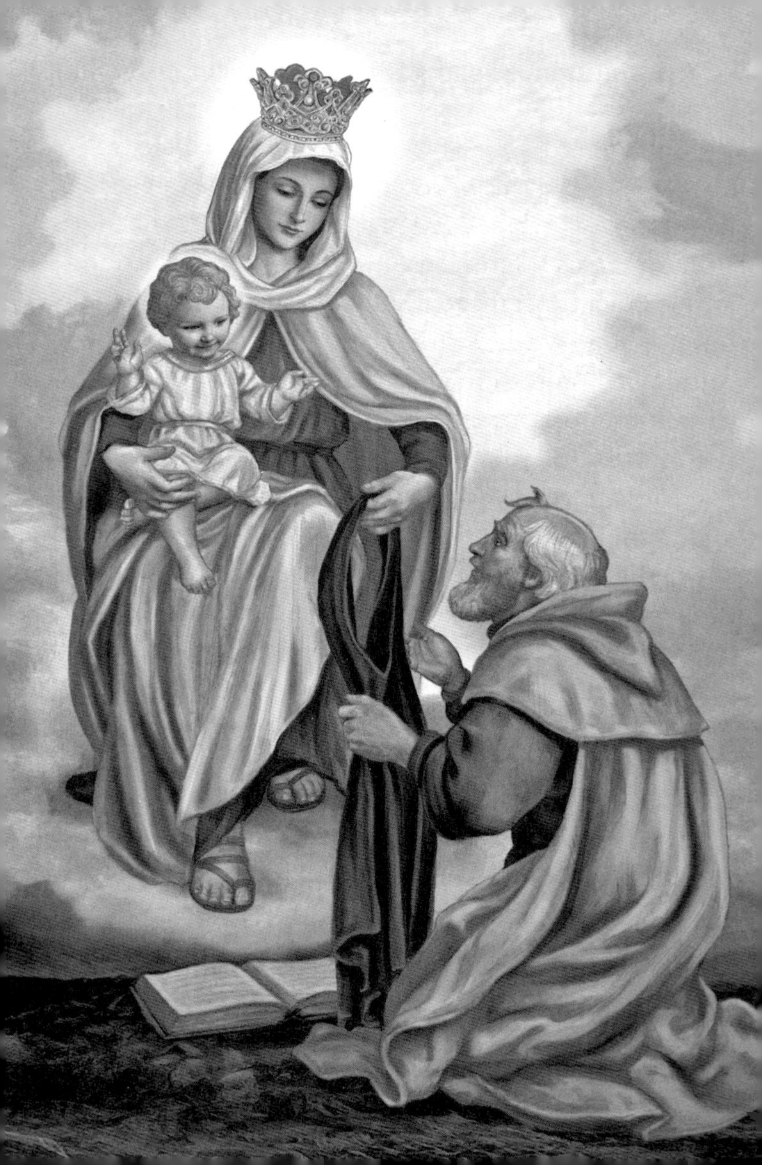

Novena to Our Lady of Mount Carmel

First Day

O Beautiful Flower of Carmel, most fruitful vine, splendor of heaven, holy and singular, who brought forth the Son of God, still ever remaining a pure virgin, assist us in our necessity! O Star of the Sea, help and protect us! Show us that you are our Mother!
(Pause and mention petitions.)

Our Lady of Mount Carmel, pray for us.

Pray one Our Father, Hail Mary and Glory Be at the end of each day's prayers.

Second Day

Most Holy Mary, Our Mother, in your great love for us you gave us the Holy Scapular of Mount Carmel, having heard the prayers of your chosen son Saint Simon Stock. Help us now to wear it faithfully and with devotion. May it be a sign to us of our desire to grow in holiness. *(Pause and mention petitions.)*

Our Lady of Mount Carmel, pray for us.

Third Day

O Queen of Heaven, you gave us the Scapular as an outward sign by which we might be known as your faithful children. May we always wear it with honor by avoiding sin and imitating your virtues. Help us to be faithful to this desire of ours. *(Pause and mention petitions.)*

Our Lady of Mount Carmel, pray for us.

Fourth Day

When you gave us, Gracious Lady, the Scapular as our Habit, you called us to be not only servants, but also your own children. We ask you to gain for us from your Son the grace to live as your children in joy, peace, and love. *(Pause and mention petitions.)*

Our Lady of Mount Carmel, pray for us.

Fifth Day

O Mother of Fair Love, through your goodness, as your children, we are called to live in the spirit of Carmel. Help us to live in charity with one another, prayerful as Elijah of old, and mindful of our call to minister to God's people. *(Pause and mention petitions.)*

Our Lady of Mount Carmel, pray for us.

Sixth Day

With loving provident care, O Mother Most Amiable, you covered us with your Scapular as a shield of defense against the Evil One. Through your assistance, may we bravely struggle against the powers of evil, always open to your Son Jesus Christ. *(Pause and mention petitions.)*

Our Lady of Mount Carmel, pray for us.

Seventh Day

O Mary, Help of Christians, you assured us that wearing your Scapular worthily would keep us safe from harm. Protect us in both body and soul with your continual aid. May all that we do be pleasing to your Son and to you. *(Pause and mention petitions.)*

Our Lady of Mount Carmel, pray for us.

Eighth Day

You give us hope, O Mother of Mercy, that through your Scapular promise we might quickly pass through the fires of purgatory to the Kingdom of your Son. Be our comfort and our hope. Grant that our hope may not be in vain but that, ever faithful to your Son and to you, we may speedily enjoy after death the blessed company of Jesus and the saints. *(Pause and mention petitions.)*

Our Lady of Mount Carmel, pray for us.

Ninth Day

O Most Holy Mother of Mount Carmel, when asked by a saint to grant privileges to the family of Carmel, you gave assurance of your Motherly love and help to those faithful to you and to your Son.

Behold us, your children. We glory in wearing your holy habit, which makes us members of your family of Carmel, through which we shall have your powerful protection in life, at death, and even after death.

Look down with love, O Gate of Heaven, on all those now in their last agony! Look down graciously, O Virgin, Flower of Carmel, on all those in need of help!

Look down mercifully, O Mother of our Savior, on all those who do not know that they are numbered among your children. Look down tenderly, O Queen of All Saints, on the poor souls! *(Pause and mention petitions.)*

Our Lady of Mount Carmel, pray for us.

Pray one Our Father, Hail Mary and Glory Be.

*One day through the Rosary
and the Scapular I will save the world.*
- Our Lady to Saint Dominic

Saint Louis Marie de Montfort and the Consecration to Mary

Saint Louis Marie de Montfort ministered as a priest and mighty preacher in early 18th century France. A man of strong temperament, Saint Louis submitted his passion to God and used it to preach the "secret of Mary"—guiding thousands of souls to Jesus through Mary. He founded the Missionaries of the Company of Mary (for priests and brothers) and the Daughters of Wisdom, whose ministry was the care of the sick.

Saint Louis wrote some renowned books, among which are *True Devotion to the Blessed Virgin*, *The Secret of Mary* and *The Secret of the Rosary*. But what was the kernel of his message?

Saint Louis wanted to present to the world a "short, easy, secure, and perfect" way to holiness, to sanctity, to pleasing God always. He believed wholeheartedly that God wants His mercy to succeed through Mary. Thus, his secret was for persons to devote themselves to Mary so that they might more fully consecrate themselves to Jesus her Son.

Jesus wants each of His followers engaged in the work of spreading the Good News—the Gospel. He told His disciples—including you and me—"All power in heaven and on earth has been given to me. Go, therefore, and make disciples of all nations, baptizing them in the name of the Father, and of the Son, and of the holy Spirit, teaching them to observe all that I have commanded you" (Matthew 28:18-20).

That being said, each of us has a different role in this great commission. And Mary's is most unique and powerful, for she is our Mother in the order of grace. Her task is to help birth, nurture, and guide us spiritually, that we, as new creations, might fulfill God's calling in our lives. In other words, God has given her the mission of helping us to become saints—great saints—that we might please God and bring others into His kingdom.

Saint Louis taught that we ought to give Mary our permission to form us into true Christians—other Christs—by the power of the Holy Spirit. In a classic analogy, he encourages us to see Mary as the mold that shapes us most surely into the image of her Son Jesus.

Pope Saint John Paul II was perhaps the most notable promoter of Saint Louis de Montfort's teaching in our time. He took as his papal motto *Totus Tuus* (Totally Yours), from De Montfort's consecration, and said that his reading of *True Devotion to the Blessed Virgin* produced a "decisive turning point" in his life.

The Saints and Mary

Mary, the first among the disciples, was the first evangelizer, bearing the Good News in the person of her unborn son to her cousin Elizabeth; she was the first disciple of Jesus, her Son and Savior. For over two millennia, Mary has also been the model of holiness for all believers. As the Catechism states, "From the Church, (the Christian) learns the *example of holiness* and recognizes its model and source in the all-holy Virgin Mary" (CCC par. 2030).

Many, many saints have enjoyed a deep love and profound respect for the Blessed Virgin Mary, and have profited greatly from her guidance and "never-failing intercession." Below are a few quotes and prayers from some of these blessed saints.

"We find ourselves on earth as in a tempestuous sea, a desert, and a vale of tears. But Mary is the Star of the Sea, the Solace of our desert, and the Light that guides us to heaven." – *Saint John Bosco*

"Mary will think of everything for us and, removing every anguish and difficulty, will quickly come to the aid of our corporal and spiritual needs."
– *Saint Maximilian Mary Kolbe*

"Do not be afraid of loving the Blessed Virgin too much. You can never love her enough. And Jesus will be very happy, because the Blessed Virgin is His Mother."
– *Saint Therese of Lisieux*

"A clean heart is a free heart. A free heart can love Christ with an undivided love in chastity, convinced that nothing and nobody will separate it from His love. Purity, chastity, and virginity created a special beauty in Mary that attracted God's attention. He showed His great love for the world by giving Jesus to her."
– *Saint Teresa of Calcutta*

"Powerful, sovereign Queen, come to our aid. Speak for us to Our Lord Jesus Christ. Who can do it better than you, who conversed so intimately with him here on earth, and now so fully possess him in Heaven? Speak to your Son for us! He cannot refuse you anything. Ask for us a great love of God, perseverance in His holy grace, and the happiness of dying in His friendship that we may see you and thank you with Him eternally. Amen." – *Saint Bernard of Clairveaux*

"Blessed Virgin Mary, who can worthily repay you with praise and thanksgiving for having rescued a fallen world by your generous consent? Accept then such poor thanks as we have to offer, unequal though they be to your merits. Receive our gratitude and obtain by your prayers the pardon of our sins. Take our prayers into the sanctuary of heaven and enable them to bring about our peace with God.

Holy Mary, help the miserable, strengthen the discouraged, comfort the sorrowful, pray for your people, plead for the clergy, intercede for all women consecrated to God. May all who venerate you, feel now your help and protection.

Make it your continual care to pray for the people of God, for you were blessed by God and were made worthy to bear the Redeemer of the world, who lives and reigns forever."– *Saint Augustine*

"Never be afraid of loving the Blessed Virgin too much. You can never love her more than Jesus did."
– *Saint Maximilian Kolbe*

"Before, by yourself, you couldn't. Now, you've turned to our Lady, and with her, how easy!"
– *Saint Josemaría Escrivá*

"We never give more honor to Jesus than when we honor his Mother, and we honor her simply and solely

to honor him all the more perfectly. We go to her only as a way leading to the goal we seek—Jesus, her Son."
– *Saint Louis Marie de Montfort*

"To give worthy praise to the Lord's mercy, we unite ourselves with Your Immaculate Mother, for then our hymn will be more pleasing to You, because She is chosen from among men and angels. Through Her, as through a pure crystal, Your mercy was passed on to us. Through Her, man became pleasing to God; Through Her, streams of grace flowed down upon us."
– *Saint Faustina*

"In dangers, in doubts, in difficulties, think of Mary, call upon Mary. Let not her name depart from your lips, never suffer it to leave your heart. And that you may obtain the assistance of her prayer, neglect not to walk in her footsteps. With her for guide, you shall never go astray; while invoking her, you shall never lose heart; so long as she is in your mind, you are safe from deception; while she holds your hand, you cannot fall; under her protection you have nothing to fear; if she walks before you, you shall not grow weary; if she shows you favor, you shall reach the goal."
– *Saint Bernard of Clairveaux*

The Popes and the Rosary

The first time the apostles met Mary, they heard her say, "Do whatever he tells you" (John 2:5). As their successors, the popes and bishops have consistently encouraged us to stay close to Our Mother.

Since the 16th century, numerous popes have promoted the Rosary, most notably Pope Leo XIII. Pope Saint Pius X developed the theme of Mary as our spiritual mother, and Pope Pius XI spoke of Mary's contribution to our redemption. In 1942, Pope Pius XII dedicated the world to Mary and within a decade declared the dogma of her Assumption. In addition, he encouraged the Family Rosary, as did his successors.

"The Rosary is the scourge of the devil."
– *Pope Adrian VI*

"Among all the devotions approved by the Church, none has been favored by so many miracles as the devotion of the most Holy Rosary." – *Pope Pius IX*

"The Rosary is...the prayer that touches most the heart of the Mother of God. Say it each day."
– *Pope Saint Pius X*

"The Rosary is a school for learning true Christian perfection."– *Pope Saint John XXIII*

Popes Saint John XXIII and Blessed Paul VI introduced new teachings on the Rosary while continuing the teachings of their predecessors. For Pope John, the Rosary was the universal prayer for all the redeemed. Additionally, he taught that the mysteries of the Rosary must have a three-fold purpose: mystical contemplation, intimate reflection, and pious intention. Pope Paul also emphasized the importance of the mysteries, saying that the prayers of the Rosary were merely an empty shell without them. Both popes continued to foster the Family Rosary through their writings and support of Father Peyton's Rosary crusade. The pontiffs showed that praying and teaching the Rosary continues to be important in our contemporary prayer life.

> The Rosary is my favorite prayer. A marvelous prayer! Marvelous in its simplicity and in its depth... Against the background of the words "Hail Mary" there pass before the eyes of the soul the main episodes in the life of Jesus Christ.... At the same time, our heart can enclose in these decades of the Rosary all the facets that make up the life of the individual, the family, the nation, the Church, and all humankind. They include personal matters and those of our neighbor, and particularly those who are closest to us. Thus in the simple prayer of the Rosary beats the rhythm of human life. – *Pope Saint John Paul II*

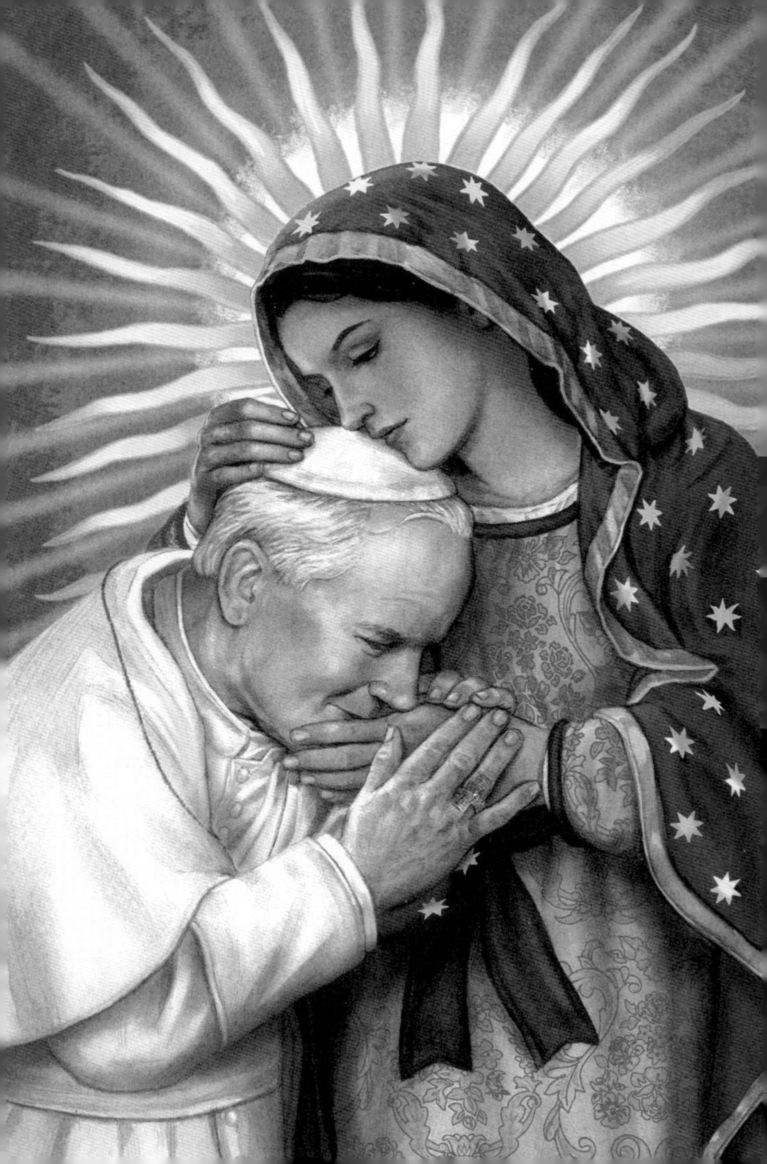

Saint John Paul II: *Totus Tuus!*

Pope Saint John Paul II enjoyed a deep, faithful love for our Blessed Mother Mary. Due in part to his profound suffering and loneliness in losing his own mother early in life, the Holy Father clung to Mary totally, as expressed in his motto, *Totus Tuus*—Totally Yours, and in the M emblazoned on his papal coat of arms.

Pope John Paul II celebrated the 25th anniversary of his pontificate by delivering his apostolic letter, *Rosarium Virginis Mariae*—The Rosary of the Virgin Mary. The Pope wrote of the Rosary, "Simple yet profound, it still remains, at the dawn of this third millennium, a prayer of great significance, destined to bring the harvest of holiness."

"With the Rosary," the Pope penned, "the Christian people sits at the school of Mary and is led to contemplate the beauty on the face of Christ and experience the depths of his love." The Holy Father gave the Church the mysteries of Light, the Luminous mysteries, and wrote that the most important reason to pray the Rosary was that it fosters a commitment to the contemplation of the Christian mystery as a very real "training in holiness."

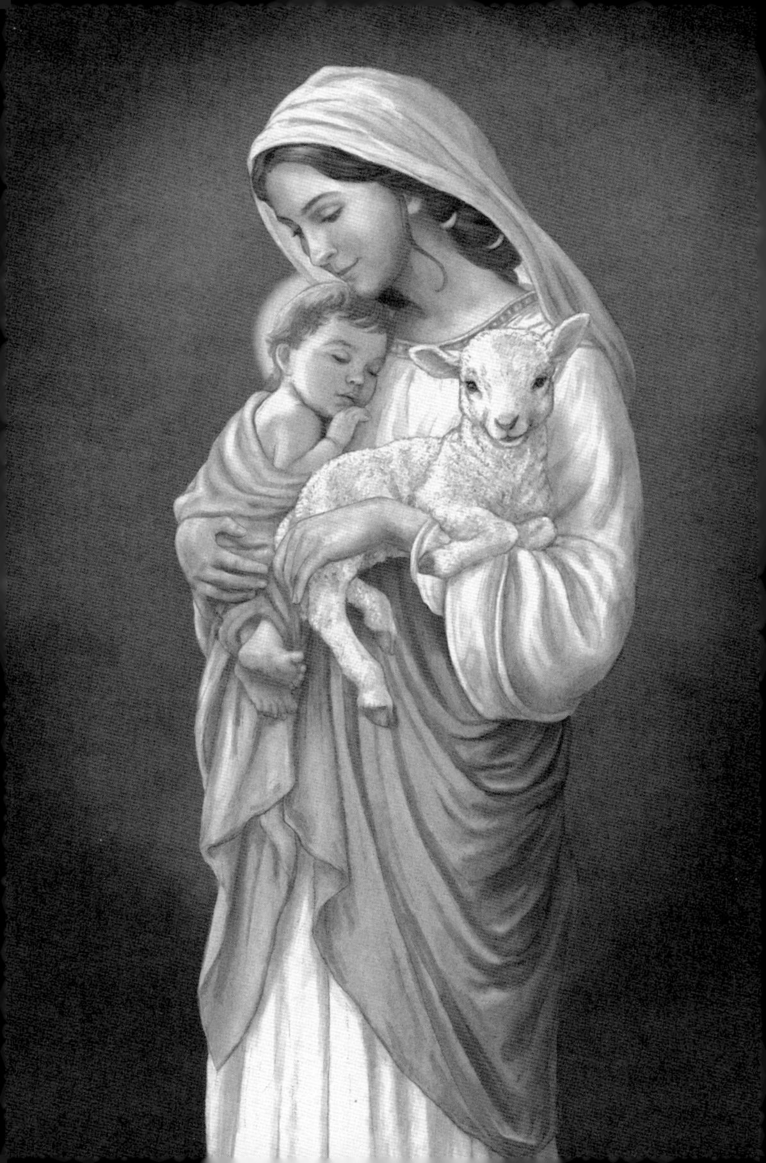

Litany of the Blessed Virgin Mary

V. Lord, have mercy. **R. Christ, have mercy.**
V. Lord, have mercy.
V. Jesus, hear us. **R. Jesus, graciously hear us.**
V. God the Father of Heaven,
R. Have mercy on us.
V. God the Son, Redeemer of the world,
R. Have mercy on us.
V. God the Holy Spirit, **R. Have mercy on us.**
V. Holy Trinity, One God, **R. Have mercy on us.**
Holy Mary, **R. Pray for us.**
Holy Mother of God,
Holy Virgin of virgins,
Mother of Christ,
Mother of divine grace,
Mother most pure,
Mother most chaste,
Mother inviolate,
Mother undefiled,
Mother most amiable,
Mother most admirable,
Mother of good counsel,
Mother of our Creator,
Mother of our Redeemer,
Mother of the Church,

Virgin most prudent, **R. Pray for us.**
Virgin most venerable,
Virgin most renowned,
Virgin most powerful,
Virgin most merciful,
Virgin most faithful,
Mirror of justice,
Seat of wisdom,
Cause of our joy,
Spiritual vessel,
Vessel of honor,
Singular vessel of devotion,
Mystical rose,
Tower of David,
Tower of ivory,
House of gold,
Ark of the Covenant,
Gate of Heaven,
Morning star,
Health of the sick,
Refuge of sinners,
Comforter of the afflicted,
Help of Christians,
Queen of angels,
Queen of patriarchs,
Queen of prophets,

Queen of apostles, **R. Pray for us.**
Queen of martyrs,
Queen of confessors,
Queen of virgins,
Queen of all saints,
Queen conceived without original sin,
Queen assumed into Heaven,
Queen of the most holy Rosary,
Queen of families,
Queen of peace,

V. Lamb of God, You take away the sins of the world,
R. Spare us, O Lord.
V. Lamb of God, You take away the sins of the world,
R. Graciously hear us, O Lord.
V. Lamb of God, You take away the sins of the world,
R. Have mercy on us.
V. Pray for us, O Holy Mother of God.
R. That we may be made worthy of the promises of Christ.

Let us pray: Grant, we beseech You, O Lord God, that we Your servants may enjoy perpetual health of mind and body, and by the glorious intercession of the Blessed Mary, ever Virgin, be delivered from present sorrow and enjoy eternal happiness. Through Christ, Our Lord. Amen.

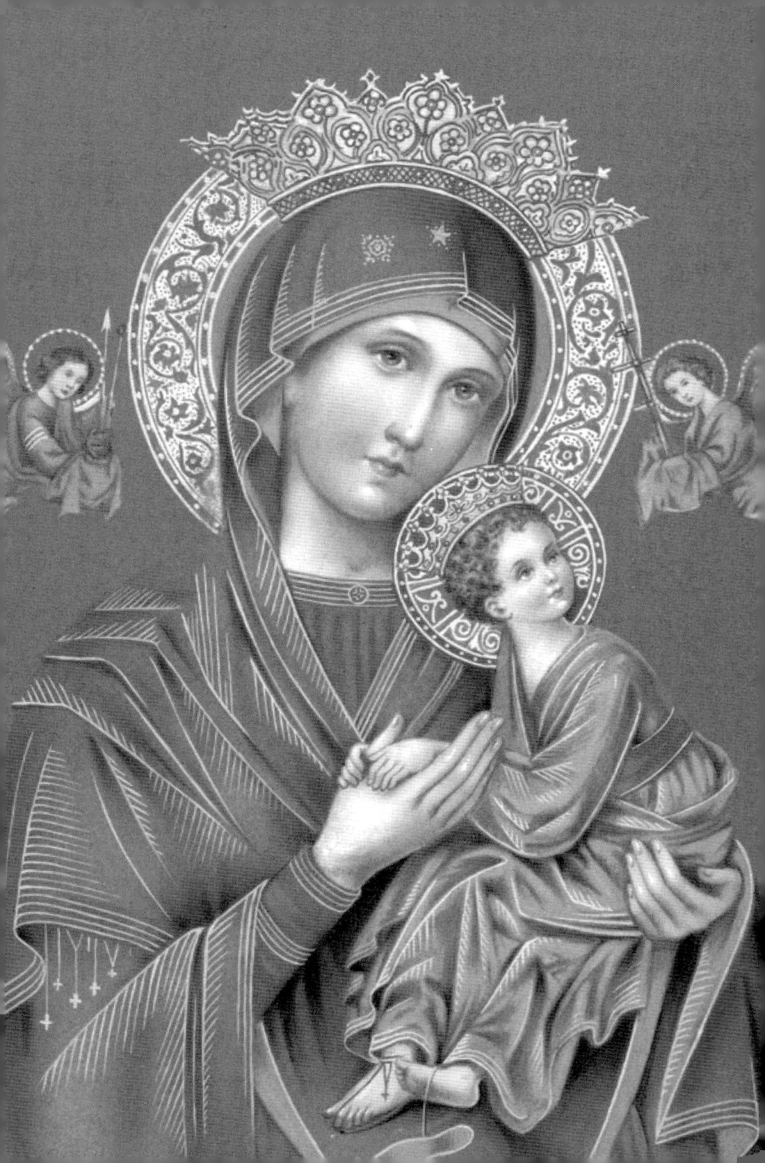

History of the Icon and the Devotion to Our Lady of Perpetual Help

The documented history of this wonder-working icon began in the year 1495, when the image was highly reverenced in a church on the island of Crete. At that time, it was already considered of great age, with some placing its origin at either the 13th or 14th century. The icon of Our Lady was afforded every measure of devotion because of the number of favors granted to those who prayed before it.

Most writers agree that the painting came into the possession of a wealthy merchant in the late 15th century. Some writers claim that the merchant stole the painting. One claims that he obtained it through honest means, while still another reports that the merchant and others fled Crete with the painting when Crete was threatened by the Turks.

Whatever the reason, it is known that the merchant carried the painting with him to Rome, and that he became seriously ill. Before he died, the merchant requested that the painting be placed in a church as soon as possible.

Contrary to his request, the painting remained in private hands until 1499, when it was transported in a solemn procession to the church of Saint Matthew. A tablet which hung for many years beside the portrait noted of this procession that, "In this manner, the picture of the most glorious Virgin Mary was enshrined in the church of Saint Matthew the Apostle, on the 27th of March, 1499, in the seventh year of the Pontificate of our most Holy Father and Lord in Christ, the Lord Pope Alexander VI."

Our Blessed Lady seemed eager to make known the virtues of her image by way of a miracle that was performed during this pageant. A man who had been paralyzed for some time was immediately cured when the image passed in procession near his home.

For the next 300 years the image hung in Saint Matthew's church, where innumerable favors were granted to the people who prayed in its chapel. With the Augustinian Order as its guardian, the image was known by various names: Our Lady of Saint Matthew, Our Lady of Never-failing Help, Our Lady of Ever-enduring Succor, and finally, Our Mother of Perpetual Help.

In 1798 Marshal Berthier, under orders from Napoleon Bonaparte, invaded Rome and forced Pope Pius VI into exile in France. One writer reports that

Berthier's successor, Massena, destroyed almost 30 churches, including the church of Saint Matthew. Thankfully, the priests had time beforehand to remove the venerated icon of our miraculous Mother Mary.

For several years the icon found refuge in the church of Saint Eusebius. It was then placed in the church of Saint Mary of Posterula, where it was hung in a side chapel and was all but forgotten for almost 40 years.

The image had at least one devoted admirer, an elderly Augustinian lay brother, Augustine Orsini. He was particularly devoted to it and often told its history to whoever would listen. One of those keenly interested was a young altar boy, Michael Marchi. When Pope Pius IX in 1853 requested that the Redemptorists establish a house in Rome, they chose a property on the Via Merula, which was located between the Lateran and Saint Mary Major.

While the church was being built, one of the priests discovered that their new church was being erected near the former site of Saint Matthew's church. Another priest asserted that he knew the history of the image and the exact location where it could be found. That priest was the former altar boy, Michael Marchi!

On learning of the portrait's whereabouts, the Redemptorist General, Father Nicholas Mauron, gained a private audience with the Holy Father. Pope Pius IX listened to Father Mauron's plan to have the portrait returned to the site where it had been enthroned for almost three centuries.

The Holy Father then recalled that as a small boy he had once prayed before the miraculous image while it was in the church of Saint Matthew.

In compliance with the wishes of the pope, the image of Our Lady was given by the Augustinians to the Redemptorist church of Saint Alphonsus. Our Lady's triumphal return to her chosen site took place on April 26, 1866. During this transfer two noteworthy cures took place: one was the healing of a boy who was seriously ill with meningitis; the other, that of a young girl who received the use of her paralyzed leg.

Never has a portrait of the Mother of God received as much papal attention as this image received from Pope Pius IX. Not only did he pray before the image as a boy, but he also approved its transfer. His approbation of the image was acknowledged on June 23, 1867, when the icon was crowned by the Vatican Chapter, in a ceremony conducted by the Latin Patriarch of Constantinople.

Pope Pius IX also fixed the feast of Our Lady of Perpetual Help for the Sunday before the feast of the Nativity of Saint John the Baptist. By a decree dated

May, 1876, he approved a special office and Mass for the Congregation of the Most Holy Redeemer (the Redemptorists).

When confraternities were erected throughout Europe, the Pope combined them in 1876 into one Archconfraternity of Our Lady of Perpetual Help and Saint Alphonsus. The Pope's name was the first in the register of the archconfraternity, and he was among the first to visit the portrait in its new home.

Devotion to this wonder-working icon spread rapidly to the United States. In 1870, when the Redemptorists were asked to establish a mission church in Roxbury, not far from Boston, they dedicated their small church to the Mother of Perpetual Help. They received from Rome the first copy of the portrait, which had been touched to the original. Since then, more than 2,300 copies similarly touched to the original have been sent to other houses of the Order.

The miraculous portrait of Our Lady of Perpetual Help is still enthroned on an altar in the church of Saint Alphonsus in Rome. The ruins of the church of Saint Matthew, where the image was reverenced for almost 300 years, are found on the grounds of the Redemptorist monastery.

Countless miracles attributed to the image extend from the time of its documented history in 1495 through the years until the present day. These seem to give ample testimony and proof of the portrait's favor with the Mother of God, Our Lady of Perpetual Help.

Novena to Our Mother of Perpetual Help

Behold at your feet, O Mother of Perpetual Help! A miserable sinner who has recourse to you and confides in you. O Mother of Mercy! Have pity on me. I hear you called by all, the Refuge and the Hope of sinners. Be then, my refuge and my hope. Assist me for the love of Jesus Christ. Stretch forth your hand to a miserable fallen creature, who commends himself to you, and who devotes himself to your service forever. I bless and thank Almighty God, who in His mercy has given me this confidence in you, which I hold to be a pledge of my eternal salvation. It is true, dearest Mother, that in the past I have miserably fallen into sin, because I had not turned to you. I know that with your help, I shall conquer. I know, too, that you will assist me, if I commend myself to you. But I fear dear Mother that in times of danger, I may forget to call on you, and thus lose my soul. This grace, then, I ask of you with all the fervor of my soul, that in all the attacks of hell, I may call on you. O Mary! Help me; O Mother of Perpetual Help, never allow me to lose my God. Amen.

Pray three Hail Marys.

O Mother of Perpetual Help, grant that I may ever invoke your powerful name, the protection of the living and the salvation of the dying. Purest Mary, let your name henceforth be ever on my lips. Delay not, Blessed Lady, to rescue me whenever I call on you. In my temptations, in my needs, I will never cease to call on you, ever repeating your sacred name, Mary, Mary. What a consolation, what sweetness, what confidence fills my soul when I utter your sacred name or even only think of you! I thank the Lord for giving you so sweet, so powerful, so lovely a name. But I will not be content with merely uttering your name. Let my love for you prompt me ever to hail you, Mother of Perpetual Help. Mother of Perpetual Help, pray for me and grant me the favor I confidently ask of you. Amen.

Pray three Hail Marys.

O Mother of Perpetual Help, you are the dispenser of all the gifts which God grants to us miserable sinners; and for this end He has made you so powerful, so rich and so bountiful, in order that you may help us in our misery. You are the advocate of the most miserable and abandoned sinners who turn to you. Come to my aid dearest Mother, for I commend myself to you. In your hands I place my eternal salvation. To you, I entrust my soul. Count me among your most devoted servants. Take me under your protection and that will be enough for me. For if you protect me dear Mother, I fear nothing; not from my sins, because you will obtain for me their pardon from Jesus your Divine Son. But one thing I fear, that in the hour of temptation, I may through negligence fail to call on you and thus perish miserably. Obtain for me, therefore, the pardon of my sins, love for Jesus, final perseverance, and the grace to turn to you, O Mother of Perpetual Help. Amen.

Pray three Hail Marys.

V. You have been made for us O Lady, a refuge.
R. A helper in need and tribulation.

V. Let us pray. O Lord Jesus Christ, You gave to us Your Mother Mary, whose renowned image we venerate, to be a Mother ever ready to help us. Grant, we beg You, that we who constantly implore her aid may merit to enjoy perpetually the fruits of Your redemption, who lives and reigns forever and ever.
R. Amen.

Prayer to the Blessed Virgin

By Saint Alphonsus

Most Holy Immaculate Virgin and my Mother Mary, to you, who are the Mother of my Lord, the Queen of the world, the Advocate, the Hope, and the Refuge of sinners, I turn today, I who am the most miserable of all.

I render you my most humble homage, O Great Queen; and I thank you for all the graces you have conferred on me until now, particularly for having delivered me from hell, which I have so often deserved.

I love you, O most Amiable Lady; and for the love which I bear for you, I promise to serve you always and to do all in my power to make others love you also. I place in you all my hopes. I confide my salvation to your care. Accept me for your servant, and receive me under your mantle, O Mother of Mercy. And since you are so powerful with God, deliver me from all temptations, or rather obtain for me the strength to triumph over them until death.

From you, I ask a perfect love for Jesus Christ. Through you, I hope to die a good death. O my Mother, by the love which you have for God, I ask you to help me at all times, but especially at the last moment of my life. Leave me not, I beg you, until you see me safe in heaven blessing you and singing of your mercy for all eternity. Amen.

Act of Consecration

Desiring to consecrate myself entirely to the service of the ever Blessed Virgin Mary, from whom after God, I expect all help and assistance in life and in death, I unite myself with the members of this pious Archconfraternity, which has been erected in honor of our Mother of Perpetual Help. And as my special patron I choose the glorious Saint Alphonsus, that he may obtain for me a true and lasting devotion to the ever Blessed Virgin, who is honored by so sweet a name. I promise, moreover, to renew my consecration to the holy Mother of God and Saint Alphonsus on the _____ day of the month or on the Sunday following, and also to receive the Holy Sacraments.

O Mother of Perpetual Help, receive me as your servant, and grant that I may experience your constant motherly assistance. I promise to have recourse to you in all my spiritual and temporal necessities. My holy patron, Saint Alphonsus, obtain for me an ardent love for Jesus Christ, and constancy in invoking our Mother of Perpetual Help. Amen.

Blessed Be Christ the King
Meditation on the Immaculate Conception

By Padre Pio, OFM, Cap.

Eternal Love, Spirit of Light and Truth, make a way into my poor mind and allow me to penetrate as far as it is possible to a wretched creature like myself, into that abyss of grace, of purity and of holiness, that I may acquire a love of God that is continually renewed, a love of God Who, from all eternity planned the greatest of all the masterpieces created by His hands: the Immaculate Virgin Mary.

From all eternity Almighty God took delight in what was to be the most perfect work of His hands, and anticipated this wonderful plan with an outpouring of His Grace. Man, created innocent, fell by disobeying Him; the mark of original sin remained engraved on his forehead and that of his progeny who will bear its consequences until the end of time.

A woman brought ruin, and a woman was to bring salvation. The one, being tempted by a serpent, stamped the mark of sin on the human race; the other was to rise through grace, pure and immaculate. She would crush the head of the serpent who was helpless before her and who struggled in vain under her heel;

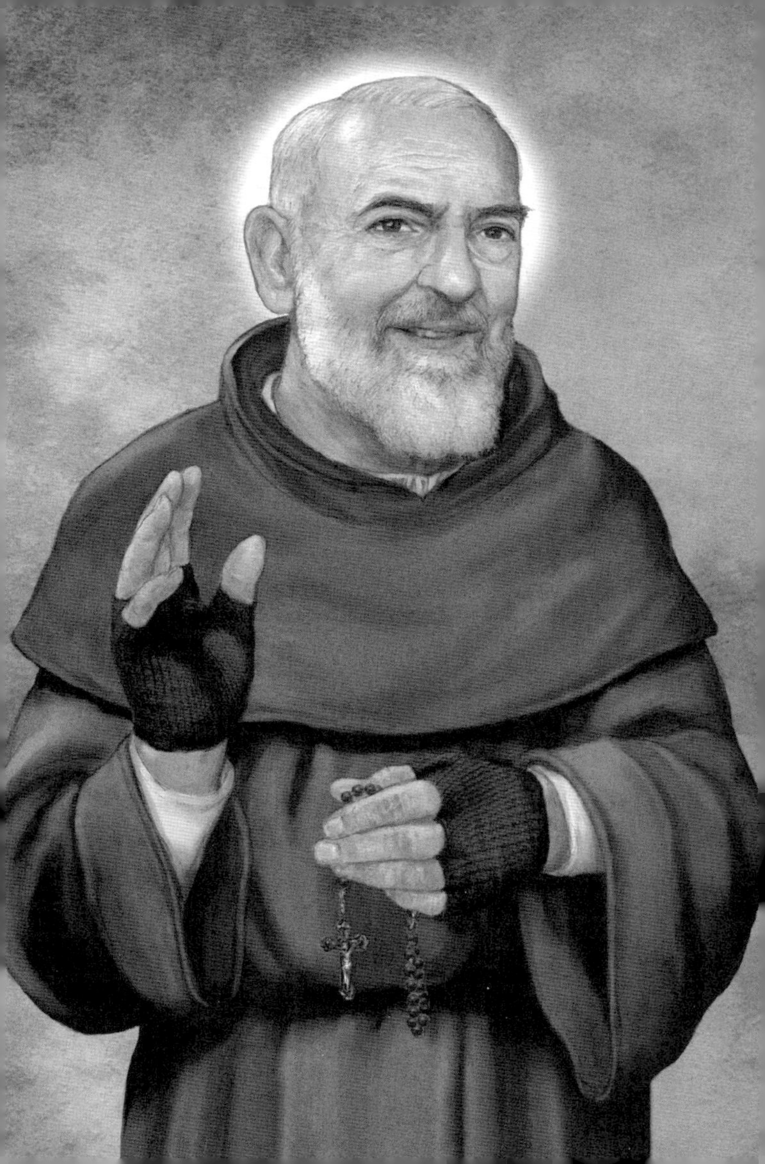

for she was conceived without sin, and through her came grace to mankind.

Protected with Grace by Him Who was to be the Savior of Mankind that had fallen into sin, she escaped all shadow of evil. She sprang from the mind of God as a pure ray of light, and will shine like a morning star over the human race that turns to her. She will be the sure guide who will direct our steps toward the Divine Sun which is Jesus Christ. He makes her radiant with divine splendor and points to her as our model of purity and sanctity. No creature surpasses her, but all creation defers to her through the Grace of Him Who made her immaculate. He Whom she was to carry in her womb was the Son of God participating with the Father and the Holy Spirit in the glory of her conception.

Clothed in light from the moment of her conception, she grew in grace and comeliness. After Almighty God, she is the most perfect of creatures; more pure than the angels; God is indeed well pleased in her, since she most resembles Him and is the only worthy repository of His secrets.

In the natural order she preceded her Divine Child, Our Lord, but in the divine order Jesus, the Divine Sun, arose before her, and she received from Him all grace, all purity and all beauty.

All is darkness compared to the pure light that renews all creation through Him Whom she bore in her womb, as the dew on the rose.

The Immaculate Conception is the first step in our salvation. Through this singular and unique gift Mary received a profusion of Divine Grace, and through her cooperation she became worthy of absorbing infinitely more.

My most pure Mother, my soul so poor, all stained with wretchedness and sin cries out to your maternal heart. In your goodness deign, I beseech you, to pour out on me at least a little of the grace that flowed into you with such infinite profusion from the Heart of God. Strengthened and supported by this grace, may I succeed in better loving and serving Almighty God Who filled your heart completely, and Who created the temple of your body from the moment of your Immaculate Conception.

The Three Divine Persons imbue this sublime creature with all her privileges, her favors and her graces, and with all of her holiness.

The Eternal Father created her pure and immaculate and is well pleased in her for she is the worthy dwelling of His only Son. Through the generating of His Son in His bosom from all eternity, He forecasts the generation of His Son as Man in the pure womb of this mother, and He clothed her from her conception in the radiant snowy garment of grace and of most perfect sanctity; she participates in His perfection.

The Son Who chose her for His Mother poured His wisdom into her that from the very beginning, by infused knowledge, she knew her God. She loved and served Him in the most perfect manner as He never until then had been loved and served on this earth.

The Holy Spirit poured His love into her; she was the only creature worthy or capable of receiving this love in unlimited measure because no other had sufficient purity to come so near to God; and being near to Him could know and love Him ever more. She was the only creature capable of containing the stream of love which poured into her from on high. She alone was worthy to return to Him from Whom came that love. This very love prepared her for that "Fiat" which delivered the world from the tyranny of the infernal enemy and overshadowed her, the purest of doves, making her pregnant with the Son of God.

Oh my Mother, how ashamed I feel in your presence, weighted down as I am with faults! You are most pure and immaculate from the moment of your conception, indeed from the moment in eternity when you were conceived in the mind of God.

Have pity on me! May one compassionate look of yours revive me, purify me and lift me up to God; raising me from the filth of this world that I may go to Him Who created me, Who regenerated me in Holy Baptism, giving me back my white stole of innocence that Original Sin had so defiled. Dear Mother, make me love Him! Pour into my heart that love that burned in yours for Him. Even though I be clothed in misery, I revere the mystery of your Immaculate Conception, and I ardently wish that through it you may purify my heart so that I may love your God and my God. Cleanse my mind that it may reach up to Him and contemplate Him and adore Him in spirit and in truth. Purify my body that I too may be a tabernacle for Him and be less unworthy of possessing Him when He deigns to come to me in Holy Communion. Amen.

We too, redeemed by Holy Baptism, are corresponding to the grace of our vocation when in imitation of our Immaculate Mother we apply ourselves incessantly to the knowledge of God in order that we may ever learn better to know Him, to serve Him and to love Him.

A Final Word

In the final moments of His agony on the cross, Jesus entrusted Mary to the care of the beloved disciple, and—by extension—all of us. It's as though Jesus were saying:

"*Behold your Mother.* I have opened for you the gates of Heaven. I have revealed to you the awesome love of My Father. I have made possible the coming of the Holy Spirit. But I am giving you something more, a final gift to help you possess the Kingdom—the gift of my own Mother, the gift of a mother's love.

"*Behold your Mother.* Look to her for love, compassion, and strength, yes, but also look to her for an example of how to follow Me with all your heart. Behold her faith, especially in contrast to the faith of your first mother, Eve. In the midst of Paradise, Eve did not believe; while, in the face of impossible circumstances, Mary did believe, and continues to help all her children believe, that God is good and that He is faithful.

"*Behold your Mother.* Never will she leave you. As you give yourself freely to her, you will find that she is very powerful, and will not rest until she has brought you, and all her children, safely home to heaven."

"*Behold your Mother!*"

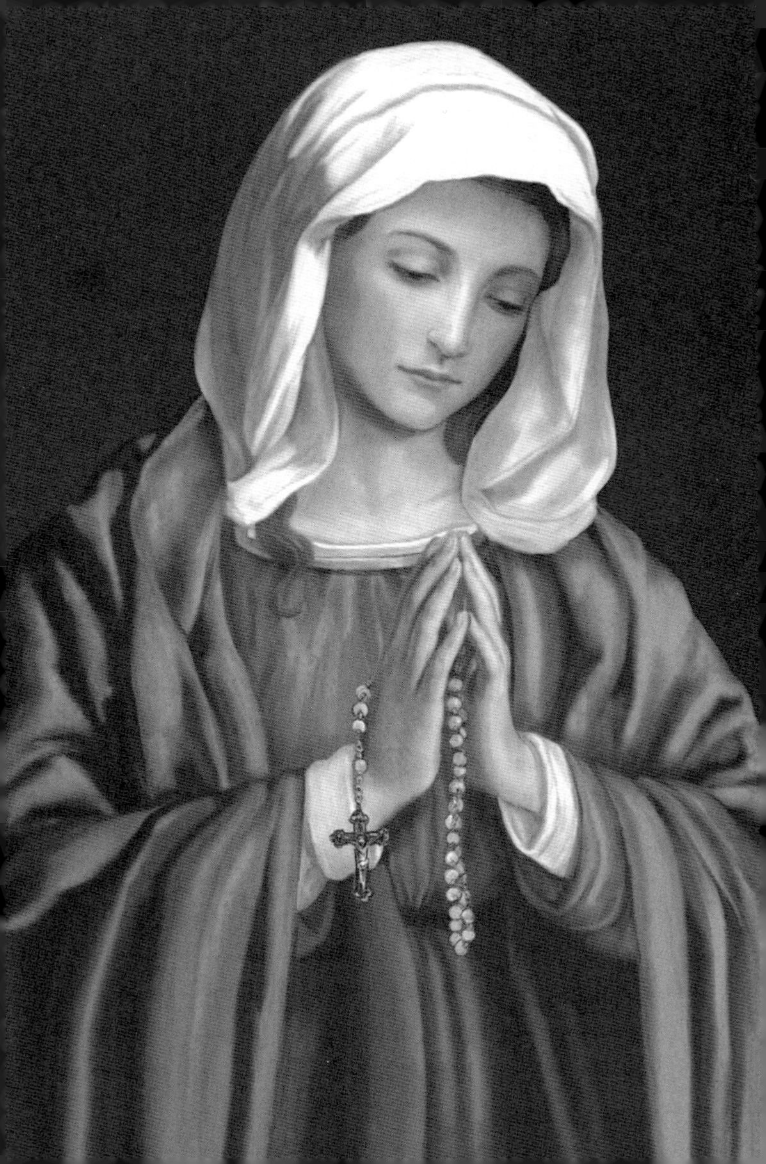

Faces of Eve
A POETIC JOURNEY OF TRANSFORMATION

Kelli Parker

Purpose Publishing
1503 Main Street #168
Grandview, Missouri 64030
www.PurposePublishing.com

Faces of Eve: A Poetic Journey of Transformation
Copyright © 2018 by Kelli Freemon Parker
ISBN: 978-0-9997999-7-0

All rights reserved. No part of this publication may be reproduced, distributed, or transmitted in any form or by any means, including photocopying, recording, or other electronic or mechanical methods, without the prior written permission of the publisher, except in the case of brief quotations embodied in critical reviews and certain other noncommercial uses permitted by copyright law.

For permission requests, write to the publisher, addressed "Attention: Permissions Coordinator," at the address above.

Bulk Ordering Information: Quantity sales. Special discounts are available on quantity purchases by churches, ministry associations, and others. For details, contact the author at FacesofEvebooks@gmail.com.

Learn more about Kelli Parker at
www.FacesofEveBooks.com

Scriptures used in this book are from the King James Version and Amplified Versions of the Bible.

Printed in the United States of America.

Dedication

For my mother and sister who walked journeys of their own, rather similar to mine. For Gigi and Yael, my biggest cheerleaders. A special thank you to my family and mentors – the women who loved me no matter my state of mind, encouraged my growth and prayed for me. And to my husband and children, who give me time to write. Thank you, Steve, for finding me at the appointed time.

Table of Transformation

Intro	6
Eve the Dreamer	7
Breathless Journey	8
On My Mind	9
All Day Long	10
In This Bed	11
The Morning After	12
The Jazz of the Rain	13
Did You Hear me Calling?	14
Your Kisses Send Me	15
Spellbound	16
Me & Mr. Jones	17
Patience	18
Temple of My Familiar	19
Good Morning, Lover	20
Diggin' On You	21
I Dream of Love	22
Mmm	23
Date Night	24
Jezebel	25
Hey Black Girl!	26
Dream Man	28
Ebony & Cream	29
Untitled	30
To Heaven and Back	32
Midnight Vamp	33
Broken-Hearted Eve, The Unraveling	34
Shackles	35
It's Better to Have Loved	36
If I knew then, What I Know Now	37
Alaiyo	38
The Break Up Song	39
Untitled	40
Invisible Woman	43

Hope for Better Days	44
Forbidden	45
Why Do I Wait?	46
Heartache	47
I Had a Bad Day	48
Dejavu	48
After Effects	49
Eve's Well Experience	50
Transformation	51
Falling in Love	52
Don't Tell me About My God	53
Addicted to His Presence	54
How Did I Reach this Place?	55
The Spirit of the Lord	56
Love Comes Softly – the Jesus Version	57
The Eyes of My Soul	58
In My Shoes – Ann's Song	59
Hindsight	60
I Trust You	62
Bits & Pieces	63
Eve the Bride	64
One More Moment	65
Falling	67
Love Glasses	68
Love Comes Softly	69
Check it Out	70
A Saved Man is a Beautiful Thing	71
Love Lingers in Time	72
Your Kisses Send Me	73
The Student	74
Winter	75
Untitled	76
Sanctuary	78
About the Author	79

Intro

WOMAN = EVE = LIFE

For centuries Woman has struggled to identify herself, where she fits in, and what her purpose is. She is led to believe that she should behave and speak in ways that are pleasing to others (Man). These ways are foreign and unnatural to her, but she gives in to the pressure to become less than she was created to be. She begins to wear the masks of allure and manipulation until she no longer recognizes herself. Unable to love and be loved, Woman must realize that she is a valuable, unique creation before she is completely used up and destroyed.

In these pages are my attempts to share Woman's journey of searching. Her desire for love takes her to places she should not be in with people who don't deserve her time or energy, let alone access to her heart. There are times that she is so sure it is true love that she gives everything. When those worlds she's built come crashing down around her, Woman lives in bitterness, anger, and depression. The gentle light of the Lord is the only thing that can bring her out. She stands before Him broken, a hopeless, empty vessel. It is then that she finds the love she's always longed for.

Eve the Dreamer

She is in love with the idea of love. She wants fairy tale, movie love that happens in an instant and lasts forever. In her quest to find that perfect love feeling, she gives too much of herself to too many, to the wrong ones, and too soon. She allows herself to be used so much that she becomes the user. The Jezebel spirit creeps in and takes over…never finding enough, never reaching a limit, never realizing what she has become.

Breathless Journey

I see you standing there
and I smile,
heart racing,
breath completely lost.
You seem a million miles away
as I hold my hand out
to meet yours.
In my mind I'm running
as fast as I can
trying to catch
up to you.
Running.
Running,
almost there,
Only a thousand miles away now
and I can see your eyes
how they sparkle,
how they dance.
Closer and closer
and closer
I'm getting.
My heart stops
as you turn
so gracefully
in my direction.
Through my smile
I whisper
a breathless hello.

On My Mind

Images,
fantasies,
dreams;
throughout the day.
Thinking of
the things you do,
the words you say.
Wide awake
or sleeping
in my bed,
I'm wondering,
hoping
thoughts of me
are in your head.
Heart flutters,
sweaty palms
when I hear
your voice,
I let you know
that I've made
my choice
to think of you
each day
and each night,
for feeling the way
I do
gives me that right.
(for Alan)

All Day Long

All day long
I wonder what you do,
what you think
are they thoughts of me,
of us?
All day long
I see your smile
your eyes shining bright
with the light of love.
All day long
I hear your voice
softly calling my name
your laughter
ringing in my ears.
All day long
I remember the gentle
warm touch of your hand
on my hand, my face.
All day long
I am a part of you
as you are of me.
All day long
my darling,
I love you more
than the day before.

In This Bed

i want to lay here
in this bed
and be silly
and giggle
and tickle
and cuddle with you.

i want to lie here
and share
and talk
of our lives before us.

i want to be here
in this bed
loving you
smelling you
feeling you.

i want to lay here
and await
the sunrise
so I can see it
wash across your
beautiful sleeping face.

i want to be here
in this bed
simply because
you are.

The Morning After

Lazily
I open my eyes
and wonder
how late I've slept.
I smile
when I realize
you're still here
engaged in angelic sleep
wrapped in a blanket
of love
that we shared
the night before.
I can't help
but wonder
if you're dreaming
of us
how we held each other
so tightly
and confessed our feelings
as we made love
through the night.
With a smile still on my lips
and you on my mind,
I drift slowly
back into my dreams.

The jazz of the Rrain

soft jazz lending its melody
to my soul
the freshness of the rain
that seems to be
cleansing my mind,
and thoughts of you . . .
I feel content and at peace
with myself
and the craziness around me.
there's something about the way
the rain falls
that makes me
want to curl up in bed
with a good book,
or let your arms swallow me up
and pull me into romantic intrigue.
the smooth overtones of jazz
spilling out of the stereo
soothing and caressing my mind
and the gentleness of the rain
forcing me to let go . . .
what else could be so sweet?

Did You Hear Me Calling?

You seemed to read my mind last night
when you showed up at my door.
I was lying there,
afraid to close my eyes,
frightened that if I did
I may never awake
to see you again
or hold you in my arms.
The darkness of the room
was swallowing me up
and I was afraid of what might be there
or what might not be.
Forcing my eyes to stay open
and my thoughts flowing,
I stared at the clock
and as if brought by my thoughts
you appeared.
I'm not afraid of the dark anymore.

Your Kisses Send Me

The softness of your lips
left me speechless
when you touched them to mine.
And when the taste of your kiss
hit me like a rush
of fresh, sweet air,
I was breathless.
I drifted way above
the clouds,
not wanting to touch
ground again,
unless you were there
to catch me,
only to send me soaring
once again
with your smile.

Spellbound

I dream
Just as you do
of the day
that we will
slip between sheets
of satin
finding memories
of the love we made
in the summer of long ago.
I wonder
just as you do
if your passion
will once again reach
all that is moist and warm
within me.
I dream
just as you do
of retracing
trails of kisses
that led to moans
and screams
and fingerprints left
on searing flesh...
I sit here
as you do
remembering and dreaming
while trying
to catch my breath.

Me & Mr. Jones

Something about you
changes everything in me
from the way I feel
to the way I breathe...

The sound of my name
falling softly from your lips
does a definite number
on the beating of my heart...

Ooh and the way you looked at me
the last time we saw each other
matched the look I hoped
I was giving you at that exact moment...

You're a good man, Mr. Jones
don't ever change that something about you
because it just so happens that I like
the something it does to me.

Patience

I like to keep you waiting
with eager anticipation
always wondering
always wanting
wanting more
of me.

I like to keep you guessing
trying to figure a way
to conjure a plan
to get closer
get closer
to my heart.

I like to keep you watching
alert and looking
for a chance
for the moment
that it's your turn
your turn
to make a move.

I like to keep you guessing
keep you waiting
because it's easier
so much easier
than admitting
that I've realized
(just this moment)
that I want you.

Temple of My Familiar

Temple of my familiar
a place that my heart called home
where my body found its resting place…
I held you close and offered
Silent apologies
For the times I hurt your heart
And made your life a circus…
But in moments
That I stand and watch the world
Going around about me,
I want to find solace
In the place
That I never really left
In the temple of my familiar
That is you

Good Morning, Lover

good morning, lover
I say as I stroke your sleeping face.
thank you for being here
to give me security and some sense
of belonging somewhere
and to someone.

good morning, lover
I say as I kiss your forehead
gently as not to wake you
and softly running my fingers
through your hair.

good morning, lover
I'll talk to you soon
over breakfast in bed.
but for now, I'll return
to my dreams and search for you there.
until then,
good morning, lover.

Diggin' on You

I'm diggin' you, baby
and all those things about you
that make me exhale slowly
letting out the slightest of moans...

I'm wantin' you, baby
and everything that comes
with the package that is you
'cause you are beautiful in my eyes...

I'm dreamin' of you, baby
and the day that I taste your kiss
as your hands are playin'
up and down my backside...

Yeah, I'm comin' to get you, baby
and all those things about you
that make me lick my lips
in sweet anticipation...

I Dream of Love

I extended my arms to you this morning
as I heard you whisper my name
I reached to pull you close to me
not knowing it was in vain.
I wanted your lips, your hands on my skin
for you to strip me till I was bare
but opened my eyes in disappointment
and did not find you there.
My dream was so vividly real
I thought you were there at my side
But your side of the bed was empty
So I hugged the pillow and cried.
My love for you will never die
Our memories I will forever keep
Knowing I can see your face
Each time I fall asleep.

Mmm

I see the mmm in you
I like the mmm that I see
when I look at you.

I feel the mmm when
I hear your voice
I like the mmm that
I feel when you talk.

I smell the mmm when
I'm close to you
I like the mmm that
I smell when you're near.

You make me mmm
and I like it
can I make you mmm too?

Date Night

In a room
filled with candles
and incense
burning 'black love'
my lover sat
massaging me
as I read
poetic whisperings
from my book
when his warm hands
reached my thighs,
my voice took on a silky tone
that played the words
like an alto sax
and sang to his soul
somehow, I knew
I would love him
for the rest of my life.

Jezebel

With one last arch
of my back
I took you
with me to a place
where only
love souls go.
My heartbeat
found its home
on top of yours,
trying to get in sync
Our eyes sent
unspoken messages
of contentment
followed by one long
sigh as we wrapped ourselves
in each other's arms
and legs and love.
It was at that moment
that I knew
I would live in that
peaceful bliss
for as long as
time would allow.

Hey Black Girl!

HEY BLACK GIRL!
(he yells at me)
COME ON OVER HERE AND LET ME
LOOK INTO THOSE DARK BROWN EYES.

HEY BLACK GIRL!
(he calls a little softer)
COME OVER HERE AND LET ME TOUCH
THOSE SOFT PINK LIPS WITH MINE.

HEY BLACK GIRL!
(he thinks he sounds sexy now)
GIRL, COME OVER HERE AND LET ME
RUN MY FINGERS ALL OVER THAT
CHOCOLATE BODY AND INHALE
YOUR WOMANLY SCENT.

HEY BLACK GIRL!
(he's back to yellin' now)
THAT SMILE OF YOURS CAN LIGHT
UP A ROOM ON THE DARKEST DAY!
COME ON OVER HERE AND LET IT
SHINE ON ME.

HEY BLACK GIRL!
(now he got that look in his eyes)
WALK ON OVER THIS WAY SO I CAN
WATCH THOSE HIPS MOVE
FROM SIDE TO SIDE.

HEY BLACK GIRL!
(now I'm finally on my way)

LET ME HEAR THE MELODY
OF THAT SOFT SEXY VOICE YOU GOT.

HEY BLACK GIRL.
(barely a whisper now)

What you want, boy?

I LOVE YOU.

Dream Man

Onyx eyes set in a diamond background
full of passion and dreams and hope
Flaring nostrils handed down from
one beautiful generation to another.
Lips, full pink softness, parting to show
a flash of brilliant perfection.
Skin of polished jet, in sharp contrast
to my caramel brown,
that glistens almost blindingly
in the sun.
Strong thighs and arms that promise
powerful and gentle holdings.
Hands carved from flawless ebony wood
and able to trace every curve
of this body from memory
feeling only like a breeze.
Soul that runs deeper than
any ocean
And a heart that knows the pain
of loving and being loved.

Ebony & Cream

You look at me
through pools of ebony and cream
and make my heart melt
like a snowflake on your tongue.
You see all the way through
to my soul, warming my body
and making me want you.
As your eyes wash over me
I can smell the heated passion
on your breath
and want you even more.
Every night I lay down to sleep
I long to dance and play there
in those pools
of ebony and cream.

Untitled

I.
Let me ride the waves
of your ecstasy
and soar over the clouds
through unexplored destinies.
Let me run my fingers
through the ins and outs
of your being
and to kiss them all
would be divine.
Let me drink in your beauty
to nourish my passion
and fuel the flame
that burns within.
Let me jump over the moon
and land with my head on your pillow
and feel your spirit enter mine
and watch them dance
as if they were one.

II.
I think of you and I smile.
Our lips me only once,
but our hearts met
the first time our eyes did,
shyly, unknowing and innocent.

I dream of our embrace
and your fingertips
making my skin
like hot silk
melting under your

passionate grasp.

Longing to feel your heart
beating against my own
making a rhythm
the world could hear
only with closed eyes.

To Heaven and Back

As I sit here in a daze,
daydreaming
thinking of all the things
I want to do to you
to make you smile,
my heart rate quickens
and my body starts to tingle.
I'm not ashamed to tell you
that I stand in front
of my mirror
and practice the way
I want to move my body
in front of and on top of you,
taking you to a high
you've never felt.
I lay in bed at night
and wonder what it was
that woman did in that movie
that made her lover scream
her name
so, I can intensify it
by a thousand,
and you can ride with me
to heaven and back.

Midnight Vamp

It is in the late-night hour
when she walks
slowly, seductively
into your dreams
teasing you with sensual words
and fingertips
painted bloody Mary,
leaving you in painful delight.

She wants to hear you
call her name
whatever it may be that day
she wants you to scream
and moan in ecstasy
and when she's done
she'll leave
quietly and unsatisfied
into the next man's fantasy.

Brokenhearted Eve – The Unraveling

She realized that she has been deceived. They do not offer their hearts to her, nor do they appreciate hers. She is broken in heart and spirit and begins a downward spiral to a dark place.

Shackles

Look into my eyes, deep into my eyes
Do you see my soul?
Do you see how lonely I really am?
How empty I feel?
A broken heart
An empty womb
Waiting to be mended
And filled
With the love of a lifetime.
If it doesn't last,
It may be better
I'll always hurt you because
I have no freedom from scars
That never heal.

You insist on prying
Into my solitary world
Trying to fix things that
Cannot be fixed,
You make me laugh and it feels good
But it is only a mask for the tears
I know will take over at nightfall
Or once everyone has gone home.
Maybe in our next lifetime
I will be your happy lover
But in this one
I can only be what I am.

It's Better to Have Loved

It's better to have loved and lost
than never to have loved at all
saying the words
believing my heart
knowing it was never in vain
the times I said
I'd love you forever
the times I watched you
walk away.
I never regretted loving you
only that it took so long
to tell you
and now you know
the ins and outs
of why and how I loved
and longed and waited
crying tears into a well
that echoed your name.
I realize now as I grow
wiser each day
that I'm much better off
not just for knowing love
but for knowing love with you.

If I Knew Then What I know Now

If I had known then
That you would captivate my heart
Then I would have never left
And torn your world apart.

If I had known then
That I'd love you the way I do
Then I would have never doubted
The desire I had for you.

If I had known then
That you'd make my life complete
Then I would have given you my all
Instead of just pieces of me.

If I had known then
That I'd love you the rest of my life
It would be me lying in your arms
And I'd be the one you'd be calling your wife.

Oh, if only I'd known it all then
Things would be different, it's true
But nothing in this world could change
The fact that I'm still in love with you.

Alaiyo

(one for whom bread is not enough)

Alaiyo
he called me
when I said
those sweet as honey kisses
were not enough
Alaiyo
my new name
when I told him
that his loving me
was simply not enough.

The Break Up Song

I had to decide
If I loved you enough,
If I loved me enough
To say goodbye one last time
I never thought
My heart would let me leave
But it was my heart
That wanted to fly
To places you would not
Allow yourself to go.

Untitled

I.
Just when you think things are going your way,
they change
And when you think things are changing,
they stay the same.
When you're in love you're brave,
putting your heart on the line,
With hope someone won't break it
just as you've done to mine.
Love is a journey
you can make only with a friend
But what happens to your heart
when that journey comes to an end?
Can you survive the lonely days
and woeful nights?
Are you so weak you'll give up
or strong enough to fight?
The ball is in your court, my love,
what will you decide to do?
Will you stay in there and fight for us
or tell me that we're through?

II.
The days seem longer
without your smile
to brighten them
or when there are
miles of silence
between us.
It seems hopeless
sometimes
when we try to fix

the earthquakes
that damn-near shatter
our relationship.
What else can we do
if our love is simply
not enough
to make us hold on?

III.
It's difficult to say goodbye
fearing I may never again witness
the sparkle in your beautiful eyes
when you laugh,
those soft lips
that part to show
flawless snow-white teeth
when you smile.
I'm afraid I will never again
feel the power of your gaze
washing over my
naked brown body
as I await you
making love to me,
or squirm under the touch
of those god-made-perfect hands
as they explore every curve
that is me.
promise me
that you'll come back.

IV.
Drifting through my mind's eye
finding you spread across the sky
calling my name.
How did you find me?
and why?
Hiding from your eyes
that seem to touch me
in places they shouldn't
and your arms
that try to create a safe home.
But you don't understand
that's not possible.

Invisible Woman

I never intended
to blend into the crowd
so that no one heard a word I said
when I decided to cry out loud.
I never meant
to be the one
to tell a man to leave his wife
only to return to her
leaving me in the middle of the night.
I never intended
to be so angry at such a young age
not knowing who or what or why
the simplest things could fuel my rage.
I never meant
to cause the pain, the lies and yes,
the tears of some
so, I will continue to fade into the background
for that is where I came from.

Hope for Better Days

Maybe tomorrow
the sun will shine again
and the birds will sing.
Maybe tomorrow
he'll come back to me
and never leave my side.
Maybe tomorrow
someone will need me
and make me feel worthwhile.
Maybe tomorrow
the tears will stop flowing
and once again I'll smile.
Maybe tomorrow
my daddy will love me
like he did before.
Or maybe
just maybe,
tomorrow
the heartache
will hurt just a little
less.

Forbidden

I've dreamed of you
Touching you
Kissing you
Hoping that it would happen
Just once,
Being close enough
and hear you whisper
That you've always
Wanted the same thing.

I can't help that I've fallen
For someone who belongs
To someone else.
The fact that you won't
Give in to my desire
Or your own
Proves what a good man
You really are.
Funny, that's one of the
Things that attracts
Me to you most.

Why Do I Wait?

Why do I wait forever
For a simple hello or to see you
Why do I wait, wondering
Hoping, believing you'll find your way
Back to me
Why do I sit alone
Waiting,
Feeling empty
Because you don't show
Why do I love you
So much
That I let you do
These things to me,
To my heart?

Heartache/ I Had a Bad Day

So many dreams
That fade
Deep into the night
Without being
Brought to life.

So many words
That remain unspoken
Because of fear
Of ridicule
Of shame.

So many hearts
Full of anguish
Of love
Of tears.

So many lives
Touched
Ruined
Taken by someone
Who doesn't give a damn.

Dejavu

It appears I'm living
The same day over and over.
The same fears, the same guilt,
The same needs.
And going through the motions
Of living life without you.
I see the same faces and
Hear those old voices
Taunting me once again.
Fear breeds insanity
And I'm gradually reaching that point.
Life doesn't seem to have the same fire,
The same intensity,
Since it doesn't include you.
Am I doomed to a lifetime
Of unseeing days and sleepless nights,
Or are you coming back to fix it?

After Effects

Alone.
Aching.
Longing for a smile,
A touch
A word.
Turning to find
Only memories
Scattered across the room
The empty space
Where your shoes
Used to rest
Hangers in the closet
Bare.
I still can't bring myself
To sleep
On your side
Of the bed
Or lay my head
Where yours once lay.
The music
Has stopped
Just as my joy
As what seems
To be
My life.

Eve's Well Experience

There is only one way to fix the brokenness. His name is Jesus. He is her salvation and savior. She looks at herself and finds forgiveness as she forgives. He is her peace.

Transformation

Transformation is
allowing God
to intervene
leaving us
stripped of shame
separated from pain and confusion
broken...
And we emerge
reshaped
rebuilt
renewed
and looking more
like Him.

Falling in Love

I've fallen in love,
been swept off my feet
by a love so awesome
that it can't be beat.
His love is gentle
His love is kind
it soothes my spirit
and consumes my mind
it heals my heart
and keeps me warm
it is my shelter
in the time of storm.
His love treats me
like I've never been treated
I feel lifted up
instead of defeated.
He caresses my face
and whispers in my ear
and when I cry
He counts every tear.
He's the best thing
to ever happen to me
It's the pure love of Jesus
He's my lover, my King.

Don't Tell Me about My God

Don't try to tell me my God ain't good,
He made me, this Earth, and every tree that ever stood.
Don't try to tell me my God don't save,
That's why we're all still here, His love doesn't change.
Don't try to tell me He ain't a miracle-workin' God
Didn't He make the ground upon which you trod?
Don't try to tell me about luck and superstition,
All that I have has come by way of divine intervention!
Don't try to tell me my God ain't good,
He's loved me more than any man ever could.
Don't try to tell me not to praise my Lord,
He made me a warrior with a shield <u>and</u> a sword
To slay those demons who try to rest in my house
Little do they know I have power to cast them out!
My God says He loves me and I claim Him as mine,
You just can't tell me He's not good…all the time.

Addicted to His Presence

I want an addiction
and I cannot lie
I want to be so caught up
that I'm always high.
I want it in me, all over me,
I've just got to have more
I want to be addicted
to the presence of the Lord.
As I hunger for Him,
I can't grow weary or tired
I want His presence,
I want that fire!
Consume me, Lord God,
take me over, make me new
Help me find that place of worship
where there's only me & you
I want that addiction,
I yearn for Him to be near
I'll fight if I have to,
just to whisper in His ear
Lord, I love you, I worship you,
I praise your holy name
When I fell in love with you,
I knew I'd never be the same.
I want to be addicted,
not because of what He gives
I want to be addicted
just because of who He is.

How Did I Reach this Place?

How did I ever reach this place
This peace,
This dream
That makes me like what I see
When I look in the mirror
And let's me be free?
How did I get here
To freedom
From the scars of shame and guilt.
To appreciate the way
My nose, my hips and mind are built?
Reminders of my past
No longer haunt me
No longer torture me
No longer keep me bound,
Because I've got new love
A new song, a new peace
That in my life abounds.

The Spirit of the Lord

The Spirit of the Lord
Surrounds me
The Spirit of the Lord
It fills me

I love the Lord and give Him praise
I lift my voice, my hands I raise
To magnify Jesus Christ
His glory, his power, his awesome might.

The spirit of the Lord
Protects me
The spirit of the Lord
It guides me.

When God gave us his only son,
Our sins were forgiven, our battles won.
He breathes his breath of life on me
I am made whole, and my soul is free.

Love Comes Softly – The Jesus Version

Love comes softly
Just as the sun
Creeps over the horizon
Caressing the earth
With warmth and light.
Jesus' love came into my life
And gently rocked me
To a place
That my heart
Calls home.
I offer myself to Him today
And offer a promise of purity
A vow of truth,
A pledge of never ending love.
Love came softly into my life
And made Jesus the lover of my soul.

The Eyes of the Soul

Eyes that fill with tears so hot
They warm the blood
Running through my veins.
Not the tears of guilt
That fell while making pleasures
With a man I thought I loved.
Not even the same tears
That came when I realized
That the very same God
That created life
And heaven and earth
Loves little old me.
But the eyes of my soul
Are crying
Releasing years of pain
And torment
With laughter and confusion
As I realize
I will
I can
I must
Survive it all
Because after all,
There is life after death.

In My Shoes – Ann's Song

You don't know me.
You think you do.
But you don't know my pain
or my joy either
for that matter.
You don't know my tears
or my unexplained laughter.
You don't know why
some days I bounce
and others, I just slide by.
Why sometimes I wish
I was invisible.
You didn't hear
the wails and moans
from my troubled, youthful mind
trying to take me back…way back.
Or how deeply my heart and soul
loved another.
You don't get why
I dance
I shout
I sing
I praise.
You don't know…
And won't know…
Even if you walked
a thousand miles
in my shoes.

Hindsight

I was a liar and a cheater
And you were an escape
From my reality
Until my reality caught up with me
And made me look in the mirror.
I couldn't love myself
And therefore, couldn't truly love you
The way you should've been loved
Or how I so badly wanted to love you.
You deserved better,
You deserved the person I was trying
So desperately to be
But instead all you got
Was my brokenness.

What should have brought us closer
Began unraveling us
And when I needed to talk
About the pain and guilt
You closed the door in my face
Leaving me to grieve alone,
And years later to finally atone
For the sins of my youth.
Years of blaming you
And hating me,
Crying rivers that fed into the ocean
Of waves that eventually became
The peaceful tide that rocked me to sleep.

Where are we now?
I am here, and you are there.
Sometimes

Like now
I wonder if you let yourself go back
And feel and see and wonder
What could've been
Or if it should've been,
If you allowed yourself to grieve
The loss of time and space and love and life…
And if it was really what we called it
Or if we tried to force the existence
Of what we thought could free us
From our solitude.

I Trust you

Whatever it takes
Whoever you use
However long
Whatever You choose

Whenever You're ready
Whatever You say
Whatever You allow
Whichever way

Whatever you do
Whatever You decide
In Your will
I choose to abide

With my life
My future too
With all my heart
In all I do

With my desires
My hopes and dreams
My plans and goals
My everything
Lord I trust You

Bits & Pieces

When I think about the peace
You've given me
And how my soul
feels free
I can't help but cry out
Your name, Jesus.

> The power of Your love
> makes my heart sing a song
> It makes me want to praise you
> All night long.

You are my peace
You are my joy
You are my everything, Lord
You are in me.

> Surround me Lord with your love
> Allow me to rest in you
> Show me the wonders of perfect peace
> And mercies that are brand new.

You are the giver of life
The reason my soul sings
I lift my hands and praise your name
Lord you are my everything.

Eve the Bride

She receives the desires of her heart and finally experiences true, pure love. She had to first fall in love with Jesus, then love herself. In the meantime, there was someone being prepared just for her.

Falling

Falling
Falling
Falling
For you
So fast
I can't seem
To stop.
I seem
To be
Losing control
Of my
Feelings
My heart.
Falling
Falling
Falling
Crazily
For you.

This poem was written at a pivotal moment in my life. I believe he was the vehicle that God used to show me that I could open my heart again. I had experienced so much pain that I'd resolved to be alone. This would be the gateway to my marriage.

In loving memory of D. T. Jones
July 2005

One Moment More

I'm just asking
For one day
One hour
One moment more
I need to hear his voice
Softly calling my name
To calm this heartache,
Ease this dreadful pain
Just one more time

It ended too soon
There was more to say
More love to give
More prayers to pray
More laughs to laugh
Just for one more day.

I know peace will come
And my tears will begin to dry
I'll think of him and smile
Instead of hearing myself cry
My friend is now in Heaven
God gave him wings to fly
Another angel watching over me
Until I join them in the sky.

But still I ask...
For one day
For one hour
For one moment more.

Love Glasses

I see you through
love-colored glasses
every dream
I ever dreamed
every man
I ever formed
in my late-night mind.

I see you through
love-colored glasses
every melody
I ever sang
every poem
I ever wrote
every lover
I ever loved.

I see you through
love-colored glasses
and thank God
for showing me beauty
for showing me truth
and sending me you.

Love Comes Softly

love comes softly
just as the sun
creeps over the horizon
caressing the earth
with warmth and light.
your love came into my life
and gently rocked me
to a place that my heart
calls home.

Check it Out

talking to you is like
finding pieces of a dream...
and your laughter tickles me
like the bubbles in champagne...
the low tone of your voice
makes me want to snuggle close
and bury my face in that place
just below your chin...

Kelli Parker

A Saved Man is a Beautiful Thing

There ain't nothin' like a saved man,
a man with the love of God in his heart,
a man that ain't afraid to cry at church
or acknowledge he needs a new start.

There ain't nothin' like a saved man,
admits his faults, repents when he's wrong
and will tell you with assurance
the word of God keeps him strong.

There ain't nothin' like a saved man,
sanctified and lifting holy hands,
ain't afraid sing from his heart
or do a holy ghost dance.

There ain't nothin' like a saved man,
a man of valor, a man of creed.
I know a few saved men like that
and they are very beautiful to me.

Love Lingers in Time

Love that lingers in time
Never fades
Just as kisses in the wind
Travel to sweet destinations.
One heart opens
To house another
To keep it warm
And full and beating.
Just as your hands
Hold my destiny
And caress my soul,
So, does my love
That lingers in you
Waiting for its chance
To once again whisper
In your ear.

Your Kisses Send Me

The softness of your lips
left me speechless
when you touched them to mine.
And when the taste of your kiss
hit me like a rush
of fresh, sweet air,
I was breathless.
I drifted way above
the clouds,
not wanting to touch
ground again,
unless you were there
to catch me,
only to send me soaring
once again
with your smile.

The Student

Teach me
The joy
The wonders
Of caring
Bring me into
Its walls
So excitingly
Daring
Teach me
To speak
Without a word
Being said
Teach me
To read
The thoughts
In your head
Show me
The beauty
Most others
Only dream of
Show me
Teach me
My darling
How to love (you)

Winter

The wind blows sharply
slapping my face
and tousling my hair.
As I pull my coat
tighter to my body
I think of home and
you by a fire
waiting for me.
I can see the excitement
in your eyes
as you prepare
something special
to surprise me upon arrival.
I think of last night,
how we gazed into each other's eyes
and confessed our love.
At last I see the familiar house
we call home,
rushing through the door
and into your arms,
feeling the chill fade
as your lips touch mine.

Untitled

I.
We have candlelit dinners
and walks in the park
long conversations and
a lot of time silence
we laugh and cry
together and apart
and grow closer
with each passing moment
we've had days go by
when we hardly speak
but we always return
to each other's arms
realizing
once again that
everything we do
is love.

II.
The thought of your smile
will forever warm me
like the feeling of
drinking champagne.
The remembrance of you
gently stroking my face
will always leave me
wanting you.
Until we meet again
on some quiet
beautiful night,
remember my kiss
and how much

I enjoyed yours.

III.
every day we live together
you touch my heart
my soul
my mind
and become
more and more
a part of my life
and part of me.
you look into my eyes
and fill me
with a burning
passion and desire
that can radiate
back to only you.

IV.
Today I found all that was
Beautiful and kind and gentle
From the soft raindrops to
The sun coming through the clouds.
Today I heard romantic melodies
From the bird's song to wind chimes
And laughter.
Today I witnessed the world
The way God intended
And it was almost perfect, almost right
The only thing missing was you.

Sanctuary

In my husband's arms
I find my sanctuary,
my heaven on earth.
I find the place that frees
me to be who I really am,
where my heart can sing
and cry and laugh,
where my touch makes a difference
and my words make him smile.
In my husband's arms
I find a place
that is my own.

About the Author

Kelli Freemon Parker is a Kansas City, Missouri native. Her love of reading and writing transformed into her hobby and passion, devoted to giving her readers exciting, emotionally charged poetry and fiction. She loves spending time with her family and working in the church. Kelli resides in South KC with her husband, Steve, and the youngest of their five children. Visit her blog for unique conversation and info on new projects.

Made in the USA
Coppell, TX
13 December 2019